Keto Air Fryer Cookbook for Beginners

1500 Days' Worth Quick & Easy Ketogenic Recipes for Weight Loss and Healthy Lifestyle

Sirena Francis

Table of contents

Introduction

The Keto diet is one of the most popular diets in the twenty-first century. People all over the world prove the effect of this way of eating day by day. The ketogenic diet originates in 1920. The diet serves as a remedy for people who suffer from diabetes and epilepsy. One more not-so-popular way of using a diet is supporting mental performance.

American Diabetes Association published studies that prove the positive effect of the keto diet on cognitive performance and preserved brain function of people with type 1 diabetes. People who suffer from Alzheimer's showed results with better memory scores. The ketogenic diet is also good for older adults who have cognitive impairment. If you experience brain fog, poor mental performance, or lack of productivity at work, the keto diet can be a great solution for you too. Besides it, the diet is perfect for people who suffer from extra weight or just want to keep fit and are looking for a diet that they can follow as a lifestyle.

Everyone hears about the ketogenic diet so much, but okay what is it exactly? Let's find out. In pursuit of perfect body shape and health, people are ready to do unbelievable things. In some cases, they just follow the trendy diet but don't have any idea what is this diet exactly and how it affects the whole body and health. A ketogenic diet is a diet with low carbohydrate intake. It means that your daily meals should include only ingredients which are rich in fats and proteins. People who follow the keto diet should maintain a low carbohydrate intake, of less than 45 grams per day. Such an eating method works the same as starvation when the body doesn't use glucose as the main energy source. Instead of it, the brain uses an alternative resource of energy, which is fat. However, before using fat the liver should turn it into ketone bodies. The ketone bodies are the main source of energy for the brain when there is a lack of glucose. The main food for the Ketogenic diet is animal fats, fish, butter, olive oil, avocado, coconut oil, and eggs. In comparison with popular Western diets the keto diet helps not only to lose weight but also to maintain the proper balance of so important for mental well-being Omega 3 and Omega 6 fatty acids whose ratio is between 1:4 and 1:3.

In this book, Professor Sirena Francis who is a nutritionist and specialist in the Ketogenic diet by profession created keto-friendly recipes which can be cooked by anyone. She wrote this cookbook intending to help thousands of people who suffer from extra weight and has health problems. She is sure that this diet can help you feel better in a short period.

Sirena Francis is sure that if you don't make the most popular mistakes while dieting – you will achieve the best results. These four mistakes are listed below.

Firstly, you should count the net carbs. Tracking your net carb will help to go into ketosis faster and get rid of excess calories.

Secondly, don't ignore the number of caloric intake. That will help you to achieve fantastic results in weight loss. Then don't ignore the keto flu which can make you sleepy, and tired, and can cause sore muscles and headaches. To ease the keto symptoms you should sleep more and drink more water. The last mistake is not eating vegetables. When you follow the keto diet, it doesn't mean you should avoid vegetables. There is so huge number of keto-friendly vegetables such as broccoli, olives, fennel, peppers, Brussels sprouts, cauliflower, etc. If you follow the simple keto rules and cook the meals from this cookbook, for sure you will achieve the greatest results in a short time and can fall in love with the keto diet lifestyle.

What to Eat and Avoid on the Keto Diet

Meat and poultry

What to eat	Enjoy occasionally	What to avoid
- chicken	- bacon	- breaded meats
- duck	- ham	- processed meats
- goose	- low-fat meat, such as skinless chicken breast	
- ground beef	- sausage	
- lamb		
- ostrich		
- partridge		
- pheasant		
- pork		
- quail		
- turkey		
- venison		

Dairy

What to eat	What to avoid
- butter	- fat-free yogurt
- cheese (soft and hard)	- low-fat cheese
- full-fat yogurt	- milk
- heavy cream	- skim milk
- sour cream	- skim mozzarella
	- sweetened yogurt

Fish and Seafood

What to eat	Enjoy occasionally	What to avoid
- catfish	- prawns	- breaded fish
- clams	- salmon	
- cod	- sardines	
- crab	- scallops	
- halibut	- shrimp	
- herring	- snapper	
- lobster	- swordfish	
- mackerel	- tilapia	
- Mahi Mahi	- trout	
- mussels	- tuna	
- oysters		

Nuts and Seeds

What to eat		What to avoid
- almonds	- peanuts	- cashews
- chia seeds	- pecans	- pistachio
- flaxseeds	- pumpkin seeds	- chocolate-covered nuts
- hazelnuts	- walnuts	- nut butter (sweetened)
- nut butter (unsweetened)	- macadamia nuts	

Oils and fats

What to eat		What to avoid	
- avocado oil	- pumpkin seed oil	- grapeseed oil	- peanut oil
- coconut oil	- sesame oil	- canola oil	- soybean oil
- hazelnut oil	- walnut oil	- cottonseed oil	- safflower oil
- olive oil		- hydrogenated oils	- processed vegetable oils
		- margarine	

Vegetables

What to eat		What to avoid	
- asparagus	- mushrooms	- carrots	- pumpkin
- avocado	- olives	- corn	- turnips
- broccoli	- onions	- beets	- yams
- cabbage	- tomatoes	- butternut squash	- yuca
- cauliflower	- peppers	- parsnips	- other starchy vegetables
- celery	- spinach	- potatoes (both sweet and regular)	
- cucumber	- zucchini		
- eggplant	- other nonstarchy vegetables		
- leafy greens			
- lettuce			

Fruits

Enjoy occasionally	What to avoid	
- lemons	- apples	- peaches
- pomegranates	- bananas	- pears
- limes	- grapefruits	- pineapple
	- limes	- plums
	- mango	- dried fruits
	- oranges	

Berries

What to eat		What to avoid	
- blackberries	- raspberries	- cherries	- melon
- blueberries	- strawberries	- grapes	- watermelon

Condiments

What to eat	What to avoid
- herbs and spices	- BBQ sauce
- lemon juice	- hot sauces
- mayonnaise with no added sugar	- ketchup
- salad dressings with no added sugar	- maple syrup
- salt and pepper	- salad dressings with added sugar
- vinegar	- sweet dipping sauces
	- tomato sauce

Grain products

What to avoid

- baked goods	- crackers	- oats	- rice
- bread	- flour	- pasta	- wheat
- cereal	- granola	- pizza	
- corn	- muesli	- popcorn	

Beans and legumes

What to avoid

- black beans	- kidney beans	- navy beans	- pinto beans
- chickpeas	- lentils	- peas	- soybeans

Eggs

What to eat

- chicken eggs	- ostrich eggs
- duck eggs	- quail eggs
- goose eggs	

Metric Volume Conversions

US Volume Measure	Metric Equivalent
1/8 teaspoon	0.5 milliliters
1/4 teaspoon	1 milliliter
1/2 teaspoon	2.5 milliliters
3/4 teaspoon	4 milliliters
1 teaspoon	5 milliliters
1 1/4 teaspoons	6 milliliters
1 1/2 teaspoons	7.5 milliliters
1 3/4 teaspoons	8.5 milliliters
2 teaspoons	10 milliliters
1/2 tablespoon	7.5 milliliters
1 tablespoon (3 teaspoons, 1/2 fluid ounce)	15 milliliters
2 tablespoons (1 fluid ounce)	30 milliliters
1/4 cup (4 tablespoons)	60 milliliters
1/3 cup	90 milliliters
1/2 cup (4 fluid ounces)	125 milliliters
2/3 cup	160 milliliters
3/4 cup (6 fluid ounces)	180 milliliters
1 cup (16 tablespoons, 8 fluid ounces)	250 milliliters
1 1/4 cups	300 milliliters
1 1/2 cups (12 fluid ounces)	360 milliliters
1 2/3 cups	400 milliliters
2 cups (1 pint)	500 Milliliters
3 cups	700 Milliliters
4 cups (1 quart)	950 milliliters
1 quart plus 1/4 cup	1 liter
4 quarts (1 gallon)	3.8 liters

Metric Weight Conversions

US Weight Measure	Metric Equivalent
1/2 ounce	7 grams
1/2 ounce	15 grams
3/4 ounce	21 grams
1 ounce	28 grams
1 1/4 ounces	35 grams
1 1/2 ounces	42.5 grams
1 2/3 ounces	45 grams
2 ounces	57 grams
3 ounces	85 grams
4 ounces (1/4 pound)	113 grams
5 ounces	142 grams
6 ounces	170 grams
7 ounces	198 grams
8 ounces (1/2 pound)	227 grams
12 ounces (3/4 pound)	340 Grams
16 ounces (1 pound)	454 grams
32.5 ounces (2.2 pounds)	1 kilogram

Oven Temperature Conversions

Degrees Fahrenheit	Degrees Celsius	Old School
200° F	100° C	Very cool oven
250° F	120° C	Very cool oven
275° F	140° C	Cool oven
300° F	150° C	Cool oven
325° F	160° C	Very moderate oven
350° F	180° C	Moderate oven
375° F	190° C	Moderate oven
400° F	200° C	Moderately hot oven
425° F	220° C	Hot oven
450° F	230° C	Hot oven
475° F	246° C	Very hot oven

BREAKFAST RECIPES

Breakfast

Eggs and Dill Cups

Prep time: 10 minutes | **Cooking time:** 15 minutes | Servings: 4

Ingredients:

- 4 eggs
- ½ teaspoon dried dill
- ½ teaspoon dried parsley
- 1 tablespoon coconut oil

Directions

1. Beat the eggs in the mixer bowl.
2. After this, add dried dill, and dried parsley. Mix the egg mixture carefully with the help of the hand mixer.
3. Then spread 4 ramekins with the coconut oil.
4. Then pour the egg mixture in every ramekin.
5. Set the Air Fryer to 360 F.
6. Put the ramekins in the Air Fryer and close it.
7. Cook the dish for 15 minutes.
8. When the time is over – you will get tender egg mixture.
9. Remove the egg cups from the Air Fryer and serve them.

Nutritional value/serving: calories 93, fat 7.8, fiber 0, carbs 0.4, protein 5.6

Avocado Canoe

Prep time: 8 minutes | **Cooking time:** 15 minutes | Servings: 2

Ingredients:

- 1 avocado, pitted
- ¼ teaspoon ground paprika
- ¼ teaspoon salt
- 2 eggs
- 1 teaspoon coconut oil
- ¼ teaspoon flax seeds

Directions

1. Take the shallow bowl and combine the ground paprika, salt, and flax seeds together. Shake it gently to make homogeneous.
2. After this, cut the avocado into 2 parts in the shape of canoes.
3. Beat the eggs in the sepa bowls.
4. Sprinkle the eggs with the spice mixture.
5. Then place the eggs in the avocado canoes.
6. Put the avocado canoes in the Air Fryer.
7. Set the Air Fryer to 355 F and close it.
8. Cook the dish for 15 minutes. Open the Air Fryer after 10 minutes of cooking – if you like, the texture

of the eggs you can remove them or keep cooking to make the eggs solid.

Nutritional value/serving: calories 290, fat 26.4, fiber 6.9, carbs 9.2, protein 7.5

Goat Cheese Ham Hash

Prep time: 10 minutes | **Cooking time:** 10 minutes | Servings: 6

Ingredients:

- 5 oz. Goat cheese
- 10 oz. ham
- 1 tablespoon coconut oil
- 3 oz chives, chopped
- 1 teaspoon ground turmeric
- 1 egg, beaten

Directions

1. Smash goat cheese.
2. Then cut the ham into the small strips.
3. Beat the egg in the bowl and whisk it with the help of the hand whisker.
4. Add the ham strips, coconut oil, chopped chives, and coconut oil.
5. After this, sprinkle the mixture with the ground turmeric.
6. Mix it up.
7. Preheat Air Fryer to 350 F.
8. Transfer the ham mixture into 3 ramekins and top with smashed goat cheese.
9. Place the ramekins in the preheated Air Fryer and cook them for 10 minutes.
10. When the time is over – remove the ramekins from Air Fryer and mix up the ham hash with the help of the fork.
11. Serve the dish!

Nutritional value/serving: calories 219, fat 15.6, fiber 1, carbs 3.2, protein 16.5

Fluffy Eggs

Prep time: 8 minutes | **Cooking time:** 4 minutes | Servings: 2

Ingredients:

- 2 eggs
- 1 teaspoon coconut oil

Directions

1. Separate the eggs into the egg whites and the egg yolks.
2. Then whisk the egg whites with the help of the hand mixer until you get strong white peaks.
3. After this, spread the Air Fryer basket tray with the coconut oil.
4. Preheat the Air Fryer to 300 F.

5. Make the medium clouds from the egg white peaks in the prepared Air Fryer basket tray.
6. Place the basket tray in the Air Fryer and cook the cloud eggs for 2 minutes.
7. After this, remove the basket from the Air Fryer, place the egg yolks in the center of every egg cloud, and return the basket back in the Air Fryer.
8. Cook the dish for 2 minutes more.
9. After this, remove the cooked dish from the basket and serve.
10. Enjoy!

Nutritional value/serving: calories 82, fat 6.6, fiber 0, carbs 0.3, protein 5.5

Bacon Cups

Prep time: 10 minutes | **Cooking time:** 12 minutes | **Servings:** 2

Ingredients:

- 2 eggs
- 4 oz. bacon
- ½ teaspoon coconut oil
- 3 oz. Cheddar cheese, shredded
- ½ teaspoon ground black pepper
- 1 tablespoon chives

Directions

1. Cho the bacon into the tiny pieces and sprinkle it with the ground black pepper.
2. Mix the chopped bacon with the help of the fingertips.
3. After this, spread the ramekins with the coconut oil and beat the eggs there.
4. Add the shredded cheese and chives.
5. After this, put the chopped bacon over the chives.
6. Put the ramekins in the Air Fryer basket and preheat the air fryer to 360 F.
7. Put the air fryer basket with the ramekins in the air fryer and cook the breakfast for 12 minutes.
8. When the time is over – remove the ramekins from the air fryer and chill them little.
9. Remove the bacon egg cups from the ramekins carefully.

Nutritional value/serving: calories 553, fat 43.3, fiber 0.2, carbs 2.1, protein 37.2

Meat Rolls

Prep time: 15 minutes | **Cooking time:** 8 minutes | **Servings:** 6

Ingredients:

- ½ cup coconut flour
- ¼ cup water
- 1 teaspoon salt
- 1 egg
- 7 oz. ground beef
- 1 tablespoon coconut oil

Directions

1. Preheat the water until it starts to boil.
2. Then combine the coconut flour with the salt and stir it.
3. Add the boiling water and whisk it carefully until the mixture is homogenous.
4. Then knead the smooth and soft dough.
5. Leave the dough.
6. Put the ground beef in the pan.
7. Roast the meat for 5 minutes on the medium heat. Stir it frequently.
8. After this beat the egg in the meat mixture and scramble it.
9. Cook the ground beef mixture for 4 minutes more.
10. Then roll the dough and cut it into the 6 squares.
11. Put the ground beef in the every square.
12. Roll the squares to make the dough sticks.
13. Sprinkle the dough sticks with the olive oil.
14. After this, put the prepared dough sticks in the air fryer basket.
15. Preheat the air fryer to 350 F and put the meat rolls there.
16. Cook the dish for 8 minutes.
17. When the meat rolls are cooked – transfer them directly to the serving plates.

Nutritional value/serving: calories 131, fat 6.1, fiber 4, carbs 6.7, protein 12.3

Cauliflower Cakes

Prep time: 10 minutes | **Cooking time:** 15 minutes | **Servings:** 4

Ingredients:

- 1 tablespoon dried parsley
- 1 egg
- 10 oz. cauliflower
- 1 tablespoon almond flour
- 1 teaspoon olive oil

Directions

1. Wash the cauliflower carefully and chop it into the small pieces.
2. Then place the cauliflower in the blender and blend it well.
3. Beat the egg in the cauliflower mixture and continue to blend it for 1 minute more.
4. After this, transfer the blended cauliflower mixture in the bowl.
5. Sprinkle it with the dried parsley, almond flour, and parsley.
6. Mix it up carefully with the help of the spoon.
7. Preheat the air fryer to 355 F.

8. Then sprinkle the air fryer basket tray with the olive oil.
9. Make the small cakes from the cauliflower mixture and put them in the air fryer basket tray.
10. Close the air fryer and cook the fritters for 8 minutes.
11. After this, turn the fritters to another side and cook them for 7 minutes more.
12. When the cauliflower cakes are cooked – serve them hot!

Nutritional value/serving: calories 58, fat 3.6, fiber 2.1, carbs 4.4, protein 3.3

Chives and Egg Rolls

Prep time: 10 minutes | **Cooking time:** 8 minutes | **Servings:** 8

Ingredients:

- 6 tablespoons almond flour
- ½ teaspoon salt
- 1 teaspoon paprika
- 1 teaspoon coconut oil
- 4 eggs
- 1 teaspoon chives
- 1 tablespoon olive oil
- 2 tablespoon water, boiled, hot

Directions

1. Put the almond flour in the bowl.
2. Add salt and hot boiled water.
3. Mix it up and knead the soft dough.
4. After this, leave the dough to rest.
5. Meanwhile, crack the eggs into the bowl.
6. Add the chives and paprika.
7. Whisk it up with the help of the hand whisker.
8. Then toss the coconut oil in the pan and preheat it well.
9. Pour the egg mixture in the melted coconut oil in the shape of the pancake.
10. Then cook the egg pancake for 1 minute from each side.
11. After this, remove the cooked egg pancake and chop it.
12. Roll the prepared dough and cut it into the 4 squares.
13. Put the chopped eggs in the dough squares and roll them in the shape of the sticks.
14. Then brush the egg rolls with the olive oil.
15. Preheat the air fryer to 355 F.
16. Put the egg rolls in the basket and transfer the basket in the air fryer.
17. Cook the dish for 8 minutes.
18. When the time is over the rolls should get light brown color.

Nutritional value/serving: calories 84, fat 7, fiber 0.7, carbs 1.5, protein 3.9

Garlic Sausages

Prep time: 15 minutes | **Cooking time:** 12 minutes | **Servings:** 6

Ingredients:

- 14 oz. ground chicken
- 1 teaspoon minced garlic
- 1 teaspoon salt
- 1 teaspoon coconut oil
- 1 tablespoon coconut flour
- 1 egg
- 1 teaspoon chili flakes
- 1 teaspoon ground coriander

Directions

1. Put the ground chicken in the bowl.
2. Beat the egg in it.
3. Then mix it up with the help of the spoon.
4. After this, sprinkle the meat mixture with the minced garlic, salt, coconut flour, chili flakes, and ground coriander.
5. Mix it up to make the smooth texture.
6. Preheat the air fryer to 360 F.
7. Make the medium sausages from the ground meat mixture.
8. Sprinkle the air fryer basket tray with the melted coconut oil.
9. Then place the prepared sausages in the air fryer basket and place it in the air fryer.
10. Cook the sausages for 6 minutes.
11. After this, turn the sausages into the second side and cook them for 6 minutes more.
12. When the time is over and the sausages are cooked – let them chill little.

Nutritional value/serving: calories 149, fat 6.5, fiber 0.5, carbs 1.1, protein 20.3

Tender Breakfast Muffins

Prep time: 15 minutes | **Cooking time:** 10 minutes | **Servings:** 5

Ingredients:

- 1 cup coconut flour
- 4 tablespoons coconut oil
- 6 tablespoons almond milk
- 1 teaspoon baking soda
- 3 oz. blueberries
- ½ teaspoon salt
- 3 teaspoon Stevie
- 1 teaspoon vanilla extract

Directions

1. Put the coconut flour in the mixing bowl.
2. Add salt, stevia, and vanilla extract.
3. After this, add coconut oil and almond milk.

4. Smash the blueberries gently and add themto the coconut flour mixture.
5. Stir it carefully with the help of the fork until the mass is homogeneous.
6. After this, leave the muffin mixture for 5 minutes in warm place.
7. Meanwhile, preheat the air fryer to 400 F.
8. Prepare the muffin forms.
9. Pour the dough in the muffin forms. Fill only ½ part of every muffin form.
10. When the air fryer is preheated – put the muffing forms with the filling in the air fryer basket. Close the air fryer.
11. Cook the muffins for 10 minutes.
12. When the time is over – remove the muffins from the air fryer basket.
13. Chill them until they are warm.

Nutritional value/serving: calories 168, fat 16.4, fiber 1.9, carbs 3.2, protein 2

Spicy Cauliflower Florets

Prep time: 10 minutes | **Cooking time:** 15 minutes | **Servings:** 7

Ingredients:

• 8 oz. cauliflower florets
• 6 tablespoon coconut flour
• 1 teaspoon chili pepper
• 1 teaspoon cayenne pepper
• 1 tomato
• ½ teaspoon salt
• 1 teaspoon olive oil

Directions

1. Sprinkle the cauliflower florets with the salt.
2. After this, chop the tomato roughly and transfer it to the blender.
3. Blend it well.
4. Then add the chili pepper, cayenne pepper, and dried garlic.
5. Blend the mixture.
6. Then preheat the air fryer to 350 F.
7. Sprinkle the air fryer basket with the olive oil inside.
8. Sprinkle the cauliflower florets with the blended tomato mixture generously.
9. After this, coat the cauliflower florets in the coconut flour.
10. Place the coated cauliflower florets in the air fryer basket and cook the dish for 15 minutes.
11. Shake the cauliflower florets every 4 minutes.
12. When the cauliflower is cooked – it will have light brown color.

Nutritional value/serving: calories 68, fat 2.5, fiber 5.3, carbs 9.2, protein 2.5

Dill Soufflé

Prep time: 8 minutes | **Cooking time:** 8 minutes | **Servings:** 2

Ingredients:

• 2 eggs
• 2 tablespoons heavy cream
• 1 tablespoon dried dill
• ¼ teaspoon ground paprika
• ¼ teaspoon salt

Directions

1. Preheat the air fryer to 391 F.
2. Meanwhile, crack the eggs into the bowl and add the heavy cream.
3. Whisk the mixture carefully until you get the smooth liquid texture.
4. After this, sprinkle the egg mixture with the dried dill, ground paprika, and salt.
5. Mix it up with the help of the spoon.
6. Then take 2 ramekins and pour the soufflé mixture there.
7. Place the ramekins in the air fryer basket and cook for 8 minutes.
8. When the time is over and the soufflé is cooked – remove the ramekins from the air fryer basket and chill for 2-3 minutes.

Nutritional value/serving: calories 119, fat 10, fiber 0.3, carbs 1.8, protein 6.2

Light Pizza

Prep time: 10 minutes | **Cooking time:** 11 minutes | **Servings:** 6

Ingredients:

• 12 oz. Cheddar cheese, shredded
• 1 tomato
• 1 teaspoon paprika
• ½ teaspoon dried basil
• ½ teaspoon salt
• ½ cup coconut flour
• 1 egg
• 4 tablespoon water
• 1 teaspoon coconut oil

Directions

1. Beat the egg in the bowl and whisk it with the help of the hand whisker.
2. After this, add the coconut flour and water. Mix the mixture up carefully and after this knead the non-sticky dough.
3. Then roll the dough into the thin circle.
4. Preheat the air fryer to 355 F.
5. Spray the air fryer basket tray with the melted coconut oil and place the pizza crust there.

6. Cook it for 1 minute.
7. After this, remove the air fryer basket tray from the air fryer.
8. Slice the tomato.
9. Sprinkle the pizza crust with the sliced tomato.
10. Then put the shredded Cheddar cheese over the sliced tomatoes.
11. Sprinkle the pizza with salt, paprika, and dried basil.
12. Place the pizza back in the air fryer and cook it for 10 minutes.
13. When the time is over and the pizza is cooked – slice it into the servings.

Nutritional value/serving: calories 320, fat 22.1, fiber 7.4, carbs 13.3, protein 17.6

Almond Pudding

Prep time: 10 minutes | **Cooking time:** 4 minutes | **Servings:** 3

Ingredients:

- 1 cup chia seeds
- 1 cup organic almond milk
- 1 teaspoon stevia
- 1 tablespoon coconut, shredded, unsweetened
- 1 teaspoon coconut oil

Directions

1. Take the small ramekins and put the chia seeds there.
2. Add the almond milk and stevia.
3. Stir the mixture gently with the help of the teaspoon.
4. After this, add coconut and coconut oil.
5. Place the chia seeds pudding in the air fryer basket tray and preheat the air fryer to 360 F.
6. Cook the chia pudding for 4 minutes.
7. When the time is over – remove the ramekins with the chia pudding from the air fryer and chill it for 4 minutes.
8. After this, stir every chia pudding serving with the help of the teaspoon and serve it.

Nutritional value/serving: calories 177, fat 11.6, fiber 9.9, carbs 14.8, protein 5.1

Tender Pork Sticks

Prep time: 15 minutes | **Cooking time:** 10 minutes | **Servings:** 4

Ingredients:

- 1 teaspoon dried oregano
- ¼ teaspoon ground ginger
- 1 teaspoon nutmeg
- 1 teaspoon ground black pepper
- 10 oz. pork loin
- ½ teaspoon salt

- 1 tablespoon olive oil

Directions

1. Cut the pork loin into the thick strips.
2. Then combine the ground ginger, oregano, ground black pepper, and salt in the shallow bowl. Stir it.
3. After this, sprinkle the pork strips with the spice mixture.
4. Preheat the air fryer to 380 F.
5. Sprinkle the air fryer basket with the olive oil inside and place the pork strips (sticks) there.
6. Cook the dish for 5 minutes.
7. After this, turn the pork sticks to another side and cook for 4 minutes more.
8. Remove the pork sticks from the air fryer and serve them immediately.

Nutritional value/serving: calories 207, fat 13.6, fiber 0.4, carbs 0.9, protein 19.5

Fragrant Bacon

Prep time: 8 minutes | **Cooking time:** 10 minutes | **Servings:** 4

Ingredients:

- 8 oz. bacon
- ½ teaspoon dried basil
- ½ teaspoon salt
- ½ teaspoon ground paprika
- ½ teaspoon ground thyme
- 4 oz. Parmesan cheese

Directions

1. Slice the bacon and rub it with the dried basil, salt, ground paprika, and ground thyme from each side.
2. Leave the bacon for 2-3 minutes to make it soak the spices.
3. Meanwhile, preheat the air fryer to 360 F.
4. Place the sliced bacon in the air fryer rack and cook it for 5 minutes.
5. After this, turn the sliced bacon to another side and cook it for 5 minutes more.
6. Meanwhile, shred Parmesan cheese.
7. When the bacon is cooked – sprinkle it with the shredded cheese and cook for 30 seconds more.
8. Then transfer the cooked bacon to the plates.

Nutritional value/serving: calories 399, fat 29.8, fiber 0.2, carbs 2, protein 30.2

Coconut Tots

Prep time: 12 minutes | **Cooking time:** 3 minutes | **Servings:** 5

Ingredients:

- 8 oz. mozzarella balls
- 1 egg

- ½ cup coconut flakes
- ½ cup coconut flour
- 1 teaspoon dried oregano
- 1 teaspoon ground black pepper
- 1 teaspoon paprika

Directions

1. Beat the egg in the bowl and whisk it.
2. After this, combine the coconut flour with the oregano, ground black pepper, and paprika. Stir it carefully.
3. Then sprinkle Mozzarella balls with the coconut flakes.
4. After this, transfer the balls to the whisked egg mixture.
5. Then coat them in the coconut flour mixture.
6. Put Mozzarella balls in the freezer for 5 minutes.
7. Meanwhile, preheat the air fryer to 400 F.
8. Put the frozen cheese balls in the preheated air fryer and cook them for 3 minutes.
9. When the time is over – remove the cheese tots from the air fryer basket and chill them for 2 minutes.

Nutritional value/serving: calories 220, fat 16, fiber 5.9, carbs 10, protein 11.2

Cheese Soufflé

Prep time: 10 minutes | **Cooking time:** 8 minutes | Servings: 4

Ingredients:

- 5 oz. Cheddar cheese, shredded
- 3 eggs
- 4 tablespoon coconut cream
- 1 tablespoon dill
- 1 teaspoon parsley
- ½ teaspoon ground thyme

Directions

1. Crack the eggs into the bowl and whisk them carefully.
2. After this, add the coconut cream and whisk it for 10 seconds more.
3. Then add the dill, parsley, and ground thyme.
4. Sprinkle the egg mixture with the shredded cheese and stir it.
5. Transfer the egg mixture in 4 ramekins and put the ramekins in the air fryer basket.
6. Preheat the air fryer to 390 F and cook the soufflé for 8 minutes.
7. When the time is over and the soufflé is cooked – chill it well.

Nutritional value/serving: calories 227, fat 18.6, fiber 0.5, carbs 2.1, protein 13.5

Paprika Balls

Prep time: 10 minutes | **Cooking time:** 8 minutes | Servings: 5

Ingredients:

- 8 oz. ground chicken
- 1 egg white
- 1 tablespoon dried dill
- ½ teaspoon salt
- ½ teaspoon ground nutmeg
- 2 tablespoon coconut flour
- 1 tablespoon olive oil
- 1 teaspoon paprika

Directions

1. Whisk the egg white and combine it with the ground chicken.
2. Sprinkle the chicken mixture with the dried dill and salt.
3. After this, add the ground black pepper and paprika.
4. Stir the mass carefully using the spoon.
5. Then make the hands wet and make the small balls from the ground chicken mixture.
6. Sprinkle every sausage ball with the coconut flour.
7. Preheat the air fryer to 380 F.
8. Then spray the air fryer basket tray with the olive oil inside and put the sausage balls there.
9. Cook the dish for 8 minutes.
10. You can turn the balls into another side during the cooking to get the brown color of the each side.

Nutritional value/serving: calories 142, fat 7.1, fiber 2.3, carbs 3.9, protein 14.8

Tofu and Chives Scramble

Prep time: 15 minutes | **Cooking time:** 20 minutes | Servings: 5

Ingredients:

- 10 oz tofu cheese
- 2 eggs
- 1 teaspoon chives
- 1 teaspoon ground white pepper
- 1 teaspoon coconut oil, melted

Directions

1. Shred tofu cheese and sprinkle it with the ground white pepper and melted coconut oil.
2. Mix it up and leave for 10 minutes to marinate.
3. Meanwhile, preheat the air fryer to 370 F.
4. Then transfer the marinated shredded tofu cheese in the air fryer basket tray and cook the cheese for 13 minutes.
5. Meanwhile, beat the eggs in the bowl and whisk them.
6. When the time is over – pour the egg mixture in the

shredded tofu cheese and stir it with the help of the spatula well.

7. When the eggs start to be firm – place the air fryer basket tray in the air fryer and cook the dish for 7 minutes more.
8. After this, remove the cooked meal from the air fryer basket tray and serve it.

Nutritional value/serving: calories 140, fat 6.7, fiber 2.1, carbs 8.2, protein 7.6

Hemp Seeds Bowl

Prep time: 10 minutes | **Cooking time:** 15 minutes | **Servings:** 3

Ingredients:

- 7 tablespoons hemp seeds
- 1 tablespoon coconut oil
- ¼ teaspoon salt
- 1 teaspoon stevia
- 7 tablespoon coconut milk
- ½ teaspoon ground cinnamon

Directions

1. Place the hemp seeds in the air fryer basket.
2. Sprinkle the seeds with the salt and ground cinnamon
3. Combine the coconut milk and stevia together. Stir the liquid and pour it in the seeds mixture.
4. After this, add coconut oil.
5. Preheat the air fryer to 370 F and cook the hemp seeds porridge for 15 minutes.
6. Stir it carefully after 10 minutes of cooking.
7. When the time is over – remove the hem porridge from the air fryer basket tray and chill it for 3 minutes.

Nutritional value/serving: calories 218, fat 20.9, fiber 1.6, carbs 3.6, protein 6.7

Paprika Scrambled Eggs

Prep time: 10 minutes | **Cooking time:** 10 minutes | **Servings:** 4

Ingredients:

- 4 eggs
- 5 tablespoons heavy cream
- 1 tablespoon olive oil
- 1 teaspoon paprika
- 1 teaspoon salt
- 1 teaspoon ground black pepper
- 4 oz bacon, chopped

Directions

1. Sprinkle the bacon with salt.
2. Stir the bacon gently and put in the air fryer basket.
3. Cook the chopped bacon in the preheated to 360 F air fryer for 5 minutes.
4. Meanwhile, beat the eggs in the bowl and whisk

them using the hand whisker.
5. Sprinkle the whisked egg mixture with the paprika and ground black pepper.
6. Whisk egg mixture gently again.
7. When the time is over – put the olive oil in the chopped bacon and pour the egg mixture.
8. Add the heavy cream and cook it for 2 minutes.
9. After this, stir the mixture with the help of the spatula until you get the scrambled eggs and cook the dish for 3 minutes more.

Nutritional value/serving: calories 314, fat 26.7, fiber 0.3, carbs 1.9, protein 16.6

Bacon Hash

Prep time: 8 minutes | **Cooking time:** 8 minutes | **Servings:** 4

Ingredients:

- 1 zucchini
- 7 oz. bacon, cooked
- 4 oz. Parmesan
- 2 tablespoon coconut oil
- 1 teaspoon salt
- 1 teaspoon ground black pepper
- 1 teaspoon paprika
- 1 teaspoon cilantro

Directions

1. Chop the zucchini into the small cubes and sprinkle it with the salt, ground black pepper, paprika, and cilantro.
2. Preheat the air fryer to 400 F and toss the coconut oil in the air fryer basket tray.
3. Melt it and add the zucchini cubes.
4. Cook the zucchini for 5 minutes.
5. Meanwhile, shred Parmesan.
6. When the time is over – shake the zucchini cubes carefully and add the cooked bacon.
7. Sprinkle the zucchini mixture with the shredded cheese and cook it for 3 minutes more.

Nutritional value/serving: calories 429, fat 33.8, fiber 0.9, carbs 4, protein 28.2

Parmesan Frittata

Prep time: 10 minutes | **Cooking time:** 15 minutes | **Servings:** 6

Ingredients:

- 6 eggs
- 1/3 cup coconut cream
- 1 tomato
- 1 tablespoon coconut oil
- 6 oz. Parmesan, grated
- 1 teaspoon chili pepper

Directions

1. Beat the eggs in the air fryer basket tray and whisk them with the help of the hand whisker.
2. After this, chop the tomato.
3. Add the vegetables to the egg mixture.
4. Then pour the coconut cream.
5. Sprinkle the liquid mixture with the coconut oil and chili pepper.
6. Then add Parmesan cheese to the mixture too.
7. Stir the mixture with the silicone spatula.
8. Preheat the air fryer to 375 F and cook the frittata for 15 minutes.

Nutritional value/serving: calories 207, fat 15.9, fiber 0.5, carbs 2.6, protein 15.1

Butter Biscuits

Prep time: 15 minutes | **Cooking time:** 10 minutes | Servings: 6

Ingredients:

- 1 egg
- 1 cup coconut flour
- ½ teaspoon baking soda
- 1 tablespoon apple cider vinegar
- 3 tablespoon butter
- 4 tablespoon coconut cream
- 1 teaspoon dried basil

Directions

1. Beat the egg in the bowl and whisk it.
2. Then sprinkle the mixture with the baking soda and apple cider vinegar.
3. Add the coconut cream and dried basil. Stir it.
4. After this, add butter and coconut flour.
5. Mix it up with the help of the hand mixer.
6. When you get the smooth and liquid batter – the dough is cooked.
7. Preheat the air fryer to 400 F.
8. Pour the batter dough into the muffin molds.
9. When the air fryer is preheated – put the muffin forms in the air fryer basket and cook them for 10 minutes.
10. When the time is over and the muffins are prepared – remove them from the air fryer.
11. Chill the muffins till the room temperature.

Nutritional value/serving: calories 95, fat 9.2, fiber 1.1, carbs 2, protein 1.5

Tender Chicken Liver Pate

Prep time: 10 minutes | **Cooking time:** 10 minutes | Servings: 7

Ingredients:

- 1-pound chicken liver

- 1 teaspoon salt
- 4 tablespoon coconut oil
- 1 cup water
- 1 teaspoon ground black pepper
- ½ teaspoon dried cilantro

Directions

1. Chop the chicken liver roughly and place it in the air fryer basket tray.
2. Pour the water in the air fryer basket tray.
3. Preheat the air fryer to 360 F and cook the chicken liver for 10 minutes.
4. When the time is over – strain the chicken liver mixture to discard it from the liquid.
5. Transfer the chicken liver mixture into the blender.
6. Add the coconut oil, ground black pepper, and dried cilantro.
7. Blend the mixture till you get the pate texture.
8. Then transfer the liver pate in the bowl and serve it immediately or keep in the fridge.

Nutritional value/serving: calories 176, fat 12, fiber 0.1, carbs 0.8, protein 15.9

Ginger Hash

Prep time: 7 minutes | **Cooking time:** 9 minutes | Servings: 3

Ingredients:

- 1 teaspoon baking soda
- 1 tablespoon apple cider vinegar
- 1 teaspoon salt
- 1 teaspoon ground ginger
- 1 cup almond flour
- 5 tablespoon coconut oil
- 1 egg
- ¼ cup heavy cream

Directions

1. Combine the baking soda, salt, ground ginger, and flour in the bowl.
2. Take the separate bowl and crack the egg there.
3. Add coconut oil and heavy cream.
4. Use the hand mixer and mix the liquid mixture well.
5. Then combine the dry mixture and liquid mixture together and stir it until it is smooth.
6. Preheat the air fryer to 400 F.
7. Then pour the pancake mixture into the air fryer basket tray.
8. Cook the pancake hash for 4 minutes.
9. After this, scramble the pancake hash well and keep cooking it for 5 minutes more.

Nutritional value/serving: calories 467, fat 46.6, fiber 4.1, carbs 8.9, protein 10.1

Chives Meatloaf

Prep time: 10 minutes | **Cooking time:** 20 minutes | **Servings:** 6

Ingredients:

- 3 pounds' lean ground beef
- 6 oz chives, chopped
- 1 egg
- 1 tablespoon coconut flour
- 1 teaspoon cayenne pepper
- 1 tablespoon dried basil
- 1 teaspoon butter
- 1 teaspoon olive oil

Directions

1. Beat the egg in the big bowl.
2. Add the ground beef
3. After this, add the coconut flour, chives, cayenne pepper, dried basil, and butter.
4. Put the chopp3e chives in the ground meat mixture.
5. Use the hands to make the homogeneous meatloaf mixture.
6. Preheat the air fryer to 350 F.
7. Make the meatloaf form from the ground meat mixture.
8. Sprinkle the air fryer basket with the olive oil inside and put the meatloaf there.
9. Cook the meatloaf for 20 minutes.
10. When the time is over – let the meatloaf chill little.
11. Slice it into servings.

Nutritional value/serving: calories 464, fat 16.9, fiber 1.6, carbs 2.8, protein 16.9

Flax Meal Bowl

Prep time: 5 minutes | **Cooking time:** 8 minutes | **Servings:** 3

Ingredients:

- 2 tablespoon sesame seeds
- 4 tablespoon chia seeds
- 1 cup heavy cream
- 3 tablespoon flax meal
- 1 teaspoon stevia
- ½ teaspoon ground cinnamon

Directions

1. Preheat the air fryer to 375 F.
2. Put the sesame seeds, chia seeds, heavy cream, flax meal, stevia in the air fryer basket tray.
3. Add the ground cinnamon and cook the porridge for 8 minutes.
4. When the time is over – stir the porridge carefully and leave it for 5 minutes to rest.
5. Serve the meal in bowls.

Nutritional value/serving: calories 249, fat 23.2, fiber 6.2, carbs 8.8, protein 5

Real Keto Burger

Prep time: 10 minutes | **Cooking time:** 8 minutes | **Servings:** 4

Ingredients:

- ½ tomato
- ½ cucumber
- 8 oz. ground beef
- 4 oz. bacon, cooked
- 1 teaspoon coconut oil
- 2 oz. lettuce leaves
- 1 teaspoon ground black pepper
- ½ teaspoon salt
- ½ teaspoon dried garlic

Directions

1. Beat the egg in the bowl and add the ground beef.
2. Chop the cooked bacon and add it to the ground beef mixture.
3. After this, add the coconut oil, ground black pepper, salt, and dried garlic.
4. Mix it up carefully and make the burgers.
5. Preheat the air fryer to 370 F.
6. Place the burgers there.
7. Cook the burgers for 8 minutes on each side.
8. Meanwhile, slice the cucumber, and tomato finely.
9. Place the tomato and cucumber on the lettuce leaves.
10. When the burgers are cooked – let them chill until the room temperature and place them over the vegetables.

Nutritional value/serving: calories 279, fat 16.6, fiber 0.5, carbs 3, protein 28.2

MEAT
RECIPES

Meat Recipes

Ginger Beef Steak

Prep time: 15 minutes | **Cooking time:** 12 minutes | **Servings:** 4

Ingredients:

- 1 tablespoon coconut oil
- 2 tablespoons fresh orange juice
- 1 teaspoon lemon zest, grated
- 1-pound beef steak
- 1 teaspoon ground ginger
- 1 teaspoon dried oregano
- 1 tablespoon heavy cream

Directions

1. Combine the fresh orange juice, coconut oil, lemon zest, ground ginger, dried oregano, cream together.
2. Churn the mixture well.
3. Then beat the steak gently.
4. Brush the beefsteak with the churned orange juice carefully and leave the steak for 7 minutes to marinate.
5. After this, preheat the air fryer to 360 F.
6. Put the marinated beefsteak in the air fryer basket and cook the meat for 12 minutes. The meat should have the well-done cooked structure.

Nutritional value/serving: calories 259, fat 12, fiber 0.3, carbs 1.6, protein 34.6

Garlic Pork Ribs

Prep time: 30 minutes | **Cooking time:** 30 minutes | **Servings:** 5

Ingredients:

- 1 teaspoon cayenne pepper
- 1 teaspoon minced garlic
- 1 teaspoon mustard
- 1 teaspoon chili flakes
- 16 oz. pork ribs
- 1 teaspoon olive oil
- 1 tablespoon paprika

Directions

1. Chop the pork ribs roughly.
2. Then sprinkle the pork ribs with the cayenne pepper, minced garlic, mustard, and chili flakes.
3. Then add the olive oil.
4. Add paprika and mix the pork ribs carefully.
5. Leave the pork ribs in the fridge for 20 minutes.
6. After this, preheat the air fryer to 360 F.
7. Transfer the pork ribs in the air fryer basket and cook them for 15 minutes.
8. After this, turn the pork ribs to another side and cook the meat for 15 minutes more.

Nutritional value/serving: calories 265, fat 17.4, fiber 0.7, carbs 1.4, protein 24.5

Tender Beef Tongue

Prep time: 10 minutes | **Cooking time:** 20 minutes | **Servings:** 6

Ingredients:

- 1-pound beef tongue
- 1 teaspoon salt
- 1 teaspoon ground white pepper
- 1 teaspoon paprika
- 1 tablespoon coconut oil
- 4 cup water

Directions

1. Preheat the air fryer to 365 F.
2. Put the beef tongue in the air fryer basket tray and add water.
3. Sprinkle the mixture with the salt, ground white pepper, and paprika.
4. Cook the beef tongue for 15 minutes.
5. After this, strain the water from the beef tongue.
6. Cut the beef tongue into the strips.
7. Then toss the coconut oil in the air fryer basket tray and add the beef strips.
8. Cook the beef tongue strips for 5 minutes at 360 F.

Nutritional value/serving: calories 235, fat 14.6, fiber 0.1, carbs 0.2, protein 14.6

Basil Pork Rinds

Prep time: 10 minutes | **Cooking time:** 7 minutes | **Servings:** 4

Ingredients:

- 1-pound pork rinds
- 1 teaspoon olive oil
- ½ teaspoon salt
- 1 teaspoon dried basil
- ½ teaspoon ground nutmeg

Directions

1. Preheat the air fryer to 365 F.
2. Spray the air fryer basket tray with the olive oil inside.
3. Then put the pork rinds in the air fryer basket tray.
4. Sprinkle the pork rinds with the salt, basil, and nutmeg.
5. Mix them up gently.
6. After this, cook the pork rinds for 7 minutes.
7. When the time is over – shake the pork rinds gently.

Nutritional value/serving: calories 659, fat 41.8, fiber 0.1, carbs 0.2, protein 73

Keto Corn Beef

Prep time: 10 minutes | **Cooking time:** 19 minutes | Servings: 3

Ingredients:

- 1 bay leaf
- 1 teaspoon black pepper
- ¼ teaspoon cayenne pepper
- 1 cup water
- 1-pound minced beef
- 1 teaspoon coconut oil

Directions

1. Pour water in the mold for air fryer and add the black pepper, cayenne pepper.
2. Preheat the air fryer to 400 F and put the mold with water in the air fryer basket.
3. Add minced beef, bay leaf, and coconut oil.
4. Cook the beef mixture for 7 minutes.
5. After this, mix the meat mixture carefully with the help of the fork and cook the ground beef mixture for 8 minutes more.
6. Then remove the cooked beef from the air fryer and mix it up gently with the help of the fork again.

Nutritional value/serving: calories 296, fat 11, fiber 0.2, carbs 0.5, protein 46

Garlic Beef Stew

Prep time: 15 minutes | **Cooking time:** 23 minutes | Servings: 6

Ingredients:

- 10 oz. beef short ribs
- 1 cup water
- 5 garlic cloves
- 4 oz. green peas
- ¼ teaspoon salt
- 1 teaspoon turmeric
- 1 green pepper
- 2 teaspoon coconut oil
- ½ teaspoon chili flakes
- 4 oz. kale

Directions

1. Preheat the air fryer to 360 F.
2. Place the coconut oil in the air fryer basket tray.
3. Add the beef short ribs.
4. Sprinkle the beef short ribs with the salt, turmeric, and chili flakes.
5. Cook the beef short ribs for 15 minutes.
6. Meanwhile, remove the seeds from the green pepper and chop it.
7. Chop the kale.
8. When the time is over – pour the water in the beef short ribs.
9. Add the chopped green pepper.
10. After this, sprinkle the mixture with the green peas.
11. Peel the garlic cloves and add it to the mixture too.
12. Mix it up using the wooden spatula.
13. Then chop the kale and add it to the stew mixture.
14. Stir the stew mixture one more time and cook it at 360 F for 8 minutes more.
15. When the stew is cooked – let it rest little.

Nutritional value/serving: calories 144, fat 5.9, fiber 1.7, carbs 6.7, protein 15.6

Mustard Shredded Beef

Prep time: 15 minutes | **Cooking time:** 22 minutes | Servings: 4

Ingredients:

- 1 teaspoon thyme
- 1 teaspoon ground black pepper
- 1 teaspoon dried dill
- 1 teaspoon mustard
- 4 cup water
- 2-pound beef steak
- 1 garlic clove, peeled
- 3 tablespoon coconut oil
- 1 bay leaf

Directions

1. Preheat the air fryer to 360 F.
2. Meanwhile, combine the thyme, ground black pepper, dried dill, and mustard in the small mixing bowl.
3. After this, sprinkle the beefsteak with the spice mixture from the both sides.
4. Massage the beefsteak with the help of the fingertip to make the meat soak the spices.
5. Then pour the water in the air fryer.
6. Add the prepared beef steak and bay leaf.
7. Cook the beefsteak for 20 minutes.
8. When the time is over – strain the water and discard the beefsteak from the air fryer.
9. Shred the meat with the help of 2 forks and return it back in the air fryer basket tray.
10. Add coconut oil and cook the meat for 2 minutes at 365 F.
11. After this, mix the shredded meat carefully with the help of the fork.
12. Transfer the dish to the serving bowls.

Nutritional value/serving: calories 517, fat 24.6, fiber 0.4, carbs 1.2, protein 69.2

Beef with Zucchini Noodles

Prep time: 15 minutes | **Cooking time:** 13 minutes | **Servings:** 3

Ingredients:

- 1-pound beef brisket
- 1 teaspoon ground white pepper
- 1 tomato
- 1 teaspoon salt
- 1 zucchini
- 1 teaspoon coconut oil
- 4 tablespoon water

Directions

1. Cut the beef brisket into the strips.
2. Sprinkle the beef strips with the ground white pepper and salt.
3. After this, chop the tomato roughly and transfer it to the blender.
4. Blend it well until you get the smooth puree.
5. After this, add the coconut oil in the air fryer basket and put the beef strips there.
6. Cook the beef strips for 9 minutes at 365 F.
7. Stir the beef strips carefully after 4 minutes of cooking.
8. Meanwhile, wash the zucchini carefully and make the spirals from the vegetable with the help of the spiralizer.
9. When the time of the cooking of the meat is finished – add the zucchini spirals over the meat.
10. Then sprinkle it with the tomato puree and water.
11. Cook the dish for 4 minutes more at 360 F.
12. When the time is over and the dish is cooked – stir it gently with the help of the wooden spatula.

Nutritional value/serving: calories 310, fat 11.1, fiber 1.2, carbs 3.4, protein 46.9

Tender Ground Beef

Prep time: 10 minutes | **Cooking time:** 15 minutes | **Servings:** 3

Ingredients:

- 1-pound lean ground beef
- 1 teaspoon garlic, sliced
- 1 teaspoon ground black pepper
- ¼ cup coconut cream
- 1 teaspoon olive oil
- 2 green peppers
- 1 teaspoon cayenne pepper
- 2 teaspoon water

Directions

1. Sprinkle the ground beef with the ground black pepper.
2. Add garlic and cayenne pepper.
3. Spray the air fryer basket tray with the olive oil.
4. Preheat the air fryer to 365 F.
5. Put the spiced ground beef in the air fryer basket tray.
6. Cook the beef mixture for 3 minutes.
7. Then stir it carefully. Add water.
8. Mix it up gently and cook at the same temperature regime for 2 minutes more.
9. Meanwhile, chop the green peppers into the small pieces.
10. When the time is over – add the chopped green peppers in the air fryer too.
11. Add the coconut cream and stir it till homogenous.
12. Cook the ground beef mixture for 10 minutes more.
13. When the time is over – mash the ground beef mixture with the help of the hand blender.

Nutritional value/serving: calories 361, fat 16, fiber 2.2, carbs 5.9, protein 47.2

Liver Cakes

Prep time: 15 minutes | **Cooking time:** 10 minutes | **Servings:** 4

Ingredients:

- ½ teaspoon ground paprika
- ½ teaspoon ground coriander
- 1 teaspoon ground thyme
- 2 teaspoon coconut oil
- 2 tablespoons coconut flour
- 1 teaspoon chili flakes
- 1-pound chicken liver
- 1 egg

Directions

1. Grin the chicken liver.
2. Put the ground chicken in the mixing bowl.
3. Beat the egg in the separate bowl and whisk it.
4. Add the ground paprika, ground coriander, ground thyme, and salt in the whisked egg mixture.
5. Add the whisked egg mixture in the ground liver.
6. After this, add the coconut flour.
7. Mix it up with the help of the spoon. You should get the non-sticky liver mixture. Add more coconut flour if desired.
8. Preheat the air fryer to 360 F.
9. Then melt the coconut oil and spread the air fryer basket tray with it.
10. Make the medium size liver cakes and put them in the prepared air fryer basket tray.
11. Cook the cakes for 5 minutes on each side. The cakes sides should bea little bit crunchy.
12. When the liver cakes are cooked – let them chill little.

Nutritional value/serving: calories 256, fat 11.8, fiber 2.7, carbs 5.4, protein 30.2

Tender Beef with Lettuce Salad

Prep time: 10 minutes | **Cooking time:** 12 minutes | **Servings:** 5

Ingredients:

- 2 cup lettuce
- 10 oz. beef brisket
- 2 tablespoons olive oil
- 1 tablespoon flax seeds
- 1 cucumber
- 1 teaspoon ground black pepper
- 1 teaspoon paprika
- 2 teaspoon coconut oil
- 1 teaspoon dried dill
- 2 tablespoons coconut milk

Directions

1. Cut the beef brisket into the strips.
2. Sprinkle the beef strips with the ground black pepper, paprika, and dried dill.
3. Preheat the air fryer to 365 F.
4. Put the coconut oil in the air fryer basket tray and melt it.
5. Then add the beef strips and cook them for 6 minutes from 2 sides.
6. Meanwhile, tear the lettuce and toss it in the big salad bowl.
7. Sprinkle the lettuce with flax seeds.
8. Chop the cucumber into the small cubes and add the vegetable in the salad bowl too.
9. Sprinkle the lettuce mixture with the coconut milk and stir it using 2 wooden spatulas.
10. When the meat is cooked – let it chill until the room temperature.
11. Add the beef strips in the salad bowl.
12. Stir it gently and sprinkle the salad with the olive oil.

Nutritional value/serving: calories 205, fat 13, fiber 1.3, carbs 4.2, protein 18.2

Hot Rib Eye Steak

Prep time: 10 minutes | **Cooking time:** 13 minutes | **Servings:** 2

Ingredients:

- 1-pound rib eye steak
- 1 teaspoon ground red pepper
- ½ teaspoon chili flakes
- 3 tablespoon coconut cream
- 1 teaspoon olive oil
- 1 teaspoon lemongrass
- 1 tablespoon coconut oil
- 1 teaspoon garlic powder

Directions

1. Preheat the air fryer to 360 F.
2. Take the shallow bowl and combine the ground red pepper, chili flakes, lemongrass, and garlic powder together.
3. Shake the spices gently.
4. Then sprinkle the rib eye steak with the spice mixture.
5. Melt the coconut oil and combine it with coconut cream and olive oil. Churn the mixture.
6. Pour the churned mixture into the air fryer basket tray.
7. Then add the rib eye steak.
8. Cook the steak for 13 minutes. Do not stir the steak during the cooking.
9. When the steak is cooked – transfer it on the paper towel to make it soaks all the excess fat.

Nutritional value/serving: calories 761, fat 64.8, fiber 0.9, carbs 3, protein 41

Meatballs Bake

Prep time: 15 minutes | **Cooking time:** 21 minutes | **Servings:** 7

Ingredients:

- 1 eggplant
- 18 oz. ground chicken
- 1 teaspoon minced garlic
- 1 egg
- 1 tablespoon coconut flour
- 8 oz. Parmesan, shredded
- 2 tablespoon butter
- 1/3 cup heavy cream

Directions

1. Put the ground chicken in the big bowl.
2. Add the minced garlic.
3. Then beat the egg in the bowl with the ground chicken mixture and stir it carefully until the mass is homogeneous.
4. Then add the coconut flour and mix it.
5. Make the small meatballs from the ground chicken.
6. Preheat the air fryer to 360 F.
7. Then sprinkle the air fryer basket tray with the butter and pour the heavy cream.
8. Peel the eggplant and chop it.
9. Put the meatballs over the cream and sprinkle them with the chopped eggplant.
10. Make the layer of the shredded cheese over the chopped eggplant.
11. After this, put the dish in the air fryer and cook it for 21 minutes.
12. When the time is over – let the dish chill until the room temperature.

Nutritional value/serving: calories 322, fat 18.6, fiber 2.8, carbs 6.1, protein 33.3

Butter Pork

Prep time: 10 minutes | **Cooking time:** 11 minutes | **Servings:** 3

Ingredients:

- 1 teaspoon peppercorns
- 1 teaspoon minced garlic
- ½ teaspoon dried basil
- 1 teaspoon ground coriander
- 3 tablespoon butter
- 13 oz. pork chops

Directions

1. Rub the pork chops with the dried basil, coriander, and minced garlic.
2. Then preheat the air fryer to 365 F.
3. Put the butter and peppercorns in the air fryer basket tray. Melt the butter.
4. Then put the prepared pork chops in the melted butter.
5. Cook the pork chops for 6 minutes.
6. Then turn the pork chops into another side.
7. Cook the pork chops for 5 minutes more.
8. When the meat is cooked – dry it gently with the help of the paper towel.

Nutritional value/serving: calories 498, fat 42.1, fiber 0.2, carbs 0.8, protein 27.9

Tender Beef Bites

Prep time: 10 minutes | **Cooking time:** 22 minutes | **Servings:** 3

Ingredients:

- 2 green peppers, chopped
- 1 teaspoon olive oil
- 14 oz. Beef loin, chopped
- 2 teaspoons low-sodium tomato paste
- ½ cup water
- 2 garlic cloves, sliced
- 1 teaspoon salt
- 1 teaspoon ground black pepper
- 1 teaspoon mustard

Directions

1. Spray the air fryer basket tray with the olive oil inside.
2. Preheat the air fryer to 365 F.
3. Add the chopped green pepper and cooked the vegetables for 5 minutes.
4. Then add the chopped beef.
5. Add tomato paste and water.
6. Cook the mixture for 6 minutes more.
7. After this, add the sliced garlic cloves, salt, ground black pepper, and mustard.
8. Mix the mixture up carefully to get the homogeneous

texture.
9. Cook the meal for 16 minutes more.

Nutritional value/serving: calories 236, fat 11.5, fiber 1.7, carbs 6.7, protein 25.6

Cheese Beef Slices

Prep time: 14 minutes | **Cooking time:** 25 minutes | **Servings:** 4

Ingredients:

- 12 oz. pork loin
- 7 oz. Cheddar cheese, sliced
- 5 oz chive stems
- 1 teaspoon turmeric
- 1 teaspoon dried oregano
- 2 teaspoon butter

Directions

1. Slice the pork loin into 4 slices.
2. Sprinkle every pork slice with the turmeric and dried oregano.
3. Then spread the air fryer basket tray with the butter.
4. Put the beef slices there.
5. Dice chives.
6. Make the layer of the diced chives over the beef slices.
7. Then make the layer of Cheddar cheese.
8. Preheat the air fryer to 365 F.
9. Cook the beef slices for 25 minutes.
10. When the time is over and the pork slices are cooked – let the dish chill little to make the cheese little bit solid.

Nutritional value/serving: calories 426, fat 30.3, fiber 0.3, carbs 1.2, protein 35.7

Beef Chips

Prep time: 25 minutes | **Cooking time:** 2.5 hours | **Servings:** 2

Ingredients:

- 14 oz. beef loin
- 1 teaspoon ground red pepper
- 3 tablespoon apple cider vinegar
- 1 teaspoon garlic powder
- ¼ teaspoon liquid smoke

Directions

1. Slice the beef loin into the medium pieces and then beat every sliced beef pieces.
2. Take the bowl and combine the apple cider vinegar, ground red pepper, garlic powder, and liquid smoke.
3. Whisk it gently with the help of the fork.
4. Then transfer the beaten beef pieces in the prepared mixture and stir it well.
5. Leave the meat from 10 minutes until 8 hours for

marinating.

6. Then put the marinated beef pieces in the air fryer rack.
7. Cook the beef chips for 2.5 hours at 150 F.
8. When beef chips are cooked – transfer it to the serving plate.

Nutritional value/serving: calories 373, fat 16.7, fiber 0.4, carbs 1.7, protein 53.4

Keto Meatloaf

Prep time: 15 minutes | **Cooking time:** 25 minutes | Servings: 5

Ingredients:

- 3 tablespoon butter
- 10 oz. lean ground pork
- 7 chicken ground beef
- 1 teaspoon dried dill
- ½ teaspoon ground coriander
- 2 tablespoons almond flour
- 1 tablespoon minced garlic
- 3 oz. fresh spinach
- 1 teaspoon salt
- 1 egg
- ½ tablespoon paprika
- 1 teaspoon sesame oil

Directions

1. Put the ground pork and ground beef in the big bowl.
2. Sprinkle the ground meat mixture with the dried dill, ground coriander, almond flour, minced garlic, salt, and paprika.
3. Then grind the fresh spinach and add it to the ground meat mixture.
4. After this beat the egg in the meat mixture and mix it up until you get the smooth texture of the mixture.
5. Spray the air fryer basket tray with the olive oil.
6. Preheat the air fryer to 350 F.
7. Roll the ground meat mixture gently to make the flat layer.
8. Then put the butter in the center of the meat layer.
9. Then make the shape of the meatloaf from the ground meat mixture. Use the fingertips for this step.
10. Place the prepared meatloaf in the air fryer basket tray.
11. Cook the dish for 25 minutes.
12. When the meatloaf is cooked – let it chill well.
13. Then remove the meatloaf from the air fryer basket tray and slice into servings.

Nutritional value/serving: calories 207, fat 17.5, fiber 0.7, carbs 1.8, protein 11.6

Tender Beef Heart

Prep time: 15 minutes |· **Cooking time:** 20 minutes | Servings: 2

Ingredients:

- 1-pound beef heart
- ½ cup fresh spinach
- 1 teaspoon salt
- 1 teaspoon chili flakes
- 3 cups water
- 1 teaspoon butter

Directions

1. Prepare the beef heart for cooking: remove all the fat from it.
2. Chop the fresh spinach.
3. Combine the fresh spinach and butter together. Stir it.
4. After this, make the cut in the beef heart and fill it with the spinach-chives mixture.
5. Preheat the air fryer to 400 F.
6. Pour the waterinto the air fryer basket tray.
7. Then sprinkle the prepared stuffed beef heart with the salt and chili flakes.
8. Put the prepared beef heart in the air fryer and cook it for 20 minutes.
9. When the time is over – remove the cooked heart from the air fryer and slice it
10. Then sprinkle the air fryer slices with the remaining liquid from the air fryer.

Nutritional value/serving: calories 373, fat 16.7, fiber 0.4, carbs 1.7, protein 53.4

Tender Pulled Pork

Prep time: 15 minutes | **Cooking time:** 20 minutes | Servings: 2

Ingredients:

- 1 teaspoon ground black pepper
- ½ teaspoon paprika
- 1 teaspoon cayenne pepper
- 1/3 cup coconut milk
- 1-pound pork tenderloin
- 1 teaspoon ground thyme
- 4 cup water
- 1 teaspoon coconut oil

Directions

1. Pour the water into the air fryer basket tray.
2. Add the pork tenderloin and sprinkle the mixture with the ground black pepper, paprika, cayenne pepper.
3. Preheat the air fryer to 370 F and cook the meat for 20 minutes.
4. After this, strain the liquid and shred the meat with

the help of 2 forks.

5. Then add the coconut oil and coconut milk and mix it.
6. Cook the pulled pork for 4 minutes more at 360 F.
7. When the pulled pork is cooked – let it chill briefly.

Nutritional value/serving: calories 444, fat 20.1, fiber 1.8, carbs 4, protein 60.6

Butter Bites

Prep time: 10 minutes | **Cooking time:** 14 minutes | Servings: 4

Ingredients:

- 1-pound pork loin
- 2 eggs
- 1 teaspoon butter
- ¼ cup coconut flour
- 1 teaspoon paprika
- 1 teaspoon ground coriander
- ½ teaspoon lime zest

Directions

1. Chop the pork loin into the big cubes.
2. Then sprinkle the pork cubes with the paprika, ground coriander, and lime zest.
3. Mix the meat gently.
4. Crack the egg into the bowl and whisk it.
5. Sprinkle the meat cubes with the egg mixture.
6. Coat every pork cube in the coconut flour.
7. Preheat the air fryer to 365 F.
8. Put the butter in the air fryer basket tray and then put the pork bites there.
9. Cook the pork bites for 14 minutes.
10. Turn the pork bites into another side after 7 minutes of cooking.

Nutritional value/serving: calories 320, fat 19.1, fiber 0.5, carbs 1, protein 34

Meat Kleftiko

Prep time: 25 minutes | **Cooking time:** 30 minutes | Servings: 6

Ingredients:

- 1 teaspoon garlic powder
- 1 tablespoon dried oregano
- ½ lime
- ¼ tablespoon ground cinnamon
- 3 tablespoon butter, frozen
- 18 oz. beef loin
- 1 cup coconut cream
- 1 teaspoon bay leaf
- 1 teaspoon dried mint
- 1 tablespoon olive oil

Directions

1. Mix garlic powder with the dried oregano, and ground cinnamon.
2. Then chop the lime.
3. Sprinkle the beef with the garlic mixture.
4. Then rub it with the chopped lime.
5. Combine the coconut cream, bay leaf, and dried mint together.
6. Whisk the mixture well.
7. After this, add the olive oil and whisk it one more time more.
8. Then pour the cream mixture on the beef and stir it carefully.
9. Leave the beef for 10 minutes to marinate.
10. Preheat the air fryer to 380 F.
11. Chop the butter.
12. Then place the beef in the air fryer basket tray and sprinkle it with the remaining cream mixture.
13. Then sprinkle the meat with the chopped butter.
14. Cook the meat for 30 minutes.
15. When the time is over – remove the meat from the air fryer and sprinkle it gently with the remaining cream mixture.

Nutritional value/serving: calories 328, fat 24, fiber 1.6, carbs 4, protein 25.1

Cheddar Cheese Meatballs

Prep time: 15 minutes | **Cooking time:** 8 minutes | Servings: 4

Ingredients:

- 1-pound lean ground beef
- 5 oz. Cheddar cheese
- 1 tablespoon dried basil
- 1 large egg
- ½ teaspoon salt
- 1 teaspoon paprika
- 1 tablespoon butter
- ½ teaspoon nutmeg
- 1 teaspoon minced garlic
- ½ teaspoon ground ginger

Directions

1. Crack the egg into the bowl and whisk it.
2. Then sprinkle the whisked egg with the salt, paprika, nutmeg, and ground ginger.
3. Stir it gently and add the ground pork.
4. After this, add dried basil and minced garlic.
5. Mix the mixture up using the spoon.
6. When you get the homogenous forcemeat – make 6 medium balls.
7. Cut Cheddar cheese into 6 medium cubes.
8. Fill the beef meatballs with the cheese cubes.
9. Preheat the air fryer to 365 F.

10. Toss the butter in the air fryer basket tray and melt it.
11. Then put the beef meatballs and cook them for 8 minutes.
12. Stir the meatballs once after 4 minutes of cooking.
13. When the beef meatballs are cooked – transfer them to the plates and serve hot.

Nutritional value/serving: calories 402, fat 23.1, fiber 0.3, carbs 1.4, protein 45

Beef and Broccoli

Prep time: 10 minutes | **Cooking time:** 13 minutes | **Servings:** 2

Ingredients:

- 6 oz. broccoli
- 10 oz. beef loin
- 1 teaspoon ground coriander
- 1/3 cup water
- 1 teaspoon olive oil
- 1 teaspoon coconut oil
- 1 tablespoon flax seeds
- ½ teaspoon chili flakes

Directions

1. Cut the beef loin into the medium/convenient pieces.
2. Sprinkle the beef pieces with the ground coriander and chili flakes.
3. Mix the meat up with the help of the hands.
4. Then preheat the air fryer to 360 F.
5. Spray the air fryer basket tray with the olive oil.
6. Put the beef pieces in the air fryer basket tray and cook the meat for 7 minutes.
7. Stir it once during the cooking.
8. Meanwhile, separate the broccoli into the florets.
9. When the time is over – add the broccoli florets in the air fryer basket tray.
10. Sprinkle the ingredients with the flax seeds and coconut oil. Add water.
11. Stir it gently using the wooden spatula.
12. Then cook the dish at 365 F for 6 minutes more.
13. When the broccoli is tender – the dish is cooked.

Nutritional value/serving: calories 381, fat 19.3, fiber 3.2, carbs 6.7, protein 43.6

Bacon Bites

Prep time: 15 minutes | **Cooking time:** 14 minutes | **Servings:** 4

Ingredients:

- 1-pound beef loin
- 6 oz. bacon, sliced
- 1 teaspoon salt
- 1 teaspoon turmeric
- ½ teaspoon paprika
- 1 teaspoon olive oil
- 1 tablespoon apple cider vinegar

Directions

1. Cut the beef loin into the medium bites.
2. Then put the beef bites in the big mixing bowl.
3. Sprinkle the meat with the turmeric, salt, paprika, and apple cider vinegar.
4. Mix the beef bites carefully and leave them for 10 minutes to marinate.
5. Then wrap the beef bites in the sliced bacon.
6. Secure the beef bites with the toothpicks.
7. Preheat the air fryer to 370 F.
8. Put the prepared bacon beef bites on the air fryer tray.
9. Cook the beef bites for 8 minutes.
10. After this, turn the beef bites into another side.
11. Cook the dish for 6 minutes more.
12. When the bacon beef bites are cooked – let them in the air fryer for 2 minutes.

Nutritional value/serving: calories 450, fat 28.5, fiber 0.2, carbs 1.1, protein 46.2

Indian Style Lamb Meatballs

Prep time: 10 minutes | **Cooking time:** 14 minutes | **Servings:** 2

Ingredients:

- 1 teaspoon garlic powder
- 1 tablespoon coconut oil
- ¼ tablespoon turmeric
- 1/3 teaspoon cayenne pepper
- 1 teaspoon ground coriander
- ¼ teaspoon bay leaf
- 1-pound ground lamb
- 1 egg
- 1 teaspoon ground white pepper

Directions

1. Combine the garlic powder with the ground lamb.
2. Then sprinkle the meat mixture with the turmeric, cayenne pepper, ground coriander, bay leaf, salt, and ground white pepper.
3. Beat the egg in the meat mixture.
4. Mix it up to make the smooth mass.
5. Then preheat the air fryer to 400 F.
6. Put the coconut oil in the air fryer basket tray and melt it.
7. Then make the meatballs from the lamb mixture and place them in the air fryer basket tray.
8. Cook the dish for 14 minutes.
9. Stir the meatballs twice during the cooking.

Nutritional value/serving: calories 524, fat 25.8, fiber 0.7, carbs 2.7, protein 66.9

Cinnamon Beef Bowl

Prep time: 15 minutes | **Cooking time:** 18 minutes | **Servings:** 2

Ingredients:

- 1 tablespoon minced garlic
- 1 teaspoon ground cinnamon
- 2 tablespoon apple cider vinegar
- 1 teaspoon stevia extract
- 1 tablespoon chia seeds
- 1 teaspoon olive oil
- 1-pound lean ground beef
- 4 tablespoon water

Directions

1. Sprinkle the ground beef with the apple cider vinegar and stir the meat with the help of the spoon.
2. After this, sprinkle the ground beef with the ground cinnamon, minced garlic, and olive oil.
3. Mix it up.
4. Preheat the air fryer to 370 F.
5. Put the ground beef in the air fryer basket tray and cook it for 8 minutes.
6. After this, stir the ground beef carefully and sprinkle with the chia seeds and water.
7. Mix the dish up and cook it for 10 minutes more.
8. When the time is over – stir the dish carefully.

Nutritional value/serving: calories 454, fat 16.5, fiber 0.7, carbs 2.5, protein 69.1

Lamb Kleftiko

Prep time: 25 minutes | **Cooking time:** 30 minutes | **Servings:** 6

Ingredients:

- 1 teaspoon garlic powder
- 1 tablespoon dried basil
- ½ lime
- ¼ tablespoon ground cinnamon
- 3 tablespoon butter, frozen
- 18 oz. leg of lamb
- 1 cup heavy cream
- 1 teaspoon bay leaf
- 1 teaspoon dried mint
- 1 tablespoon olive oil

Directions

1. Combine garlic powder with the dried basil, and ground cinnamon. Mix it.
2. Then chop the lime
3. Sprinkle the leg of lamb with the garlic mixture.
4. Then rub it with the chopped lemon.
5. Combine the heavy cream, bay leaf, and dried mint together.
6. Whisk the mixture well.
7. After this, add the olive oil and whisk it one more time more.
8. Then pour the cream mixture on the leg of lamb and stir it carefully.
9. Leave the leg of lamb for 10 minutes to marinate.
10. Preheat the air fryer to 380 F.
11. Chop the butter.
12. Then place the leg of lamb in the air fryer basket tray and sprinkle it with the remaining cream mixture.
13. Then sprinkle the meat with the chopped butter.
14. Cook the meat for 30 minutes.
15. When the time is over – remove the meat from the air fryer and sprinkle it gently with the remaining cream mixture.

Nutritional value/serving: calories 303, fat 21.7, fiber 0.4, carbs 1.8, protein 24.5

Tender Bites with Gravy

Prep time: 15 minutes | **Cooking time:** 17 minutes | **Servings:** 3

Ingredients:

- 1-pound beef loin
- 1 teaspoon kosher salt
- 1 teaspoon ground white pepper
- 1 cup coconut cream
- 6 oz. white mushrooms
- 1 tablespoon coconut oil
- ½ teaspoon ground ginger
- 1 teaspoon ground turmeric
- 4 oz chive stems
- 1 garlic clove, chopped

Directions

1. Cut the beef loin into Bites and sprinkle with the kosher salt, ground white pepper, and ground turmeric.
2. Preheat the air fryer to 375 F.
3. Pour the coconut cream in the air fryer basket tray.
4. Then slice the white mushrooms and add them in the coconut cream.
5. After this, add coconut oil, ground ginger, chopped chives, and chopped garlic.
6. Cook the gravy for 5 minutes.
7. Then stir the coconut cream gravy and add the pork chops.
8. Cook the beef bites at 400 F for 12 minutes.

Nutritional value/serving: calories 517, fat 36.5, fiber 2.7, carbs 7.8, protein 44.3

Saffron Beef Loin

Prep time: 20 minutes | **Cooking time:** 15 minutes | **Servings:** 2

Ingredients:

- ½ teaspoon saffron
- 1 teaspoon sage
- 1 teaspoon garlic powder
- 1 teaspoon onion powder
- 1-pound beef loin
- 3 tablespoon butter
- 1 tablespoon fresh lemon juice

Directions

1. Combine the saffron, sage, garlic powder, and onion powder together in the shallow bowl.
2. Then shake the spices gently to make them homogenous.
3. After this, coat the beef loin in the spice mixture.
4. Sprinkle the beef loin with the apple cider vinegar.
5. Leave the beef loin for 10 minutes to marinate.
6. Meanwhile, preheat the air fryer to 320 F.
7. Put the beef loin in the air fryer tray and place the butter over the meat.
8. Cook the meat for 15 minutes.
9. When the meat is cooked – let it chill briefly.

Nutritional value/serving: calories 578, fat 36.3, fiber 0.4, carbs 2.5, protein 61.3

POULTRY
RECIPES

Poultry Recipes

Basil Chicken with Green Beans

Prep time: 5 minutes | **Cooking time:** 35 minutes | **Servings:** 4

Ingredients:

- 4 chicken breasts, skinless, boneless and halved
- 10 ounces water
- 1 teaspoon basil, dried
- 10 ounces green beans, trimmed and halved
- 2 tablespoons sesame oil
- 1 tablespoon parsley, chopped

Directions

Heat up a pan and pour the sesame oil inside.
1. Preheat it over medium-high heat, add the chicken and brown for 2 minutes on each side. Add the remaining ingredients, toss a bit.
2. Transfer the ingredients in the air fryer basket and cook at 380 degrees F for 30 minutes.

Nutritional value/serving: calories 360, fat 17.7, fiber 2.4, carbs 5.1, protein 43.6

Garlic Chicken Breasts

Prep time: 5 minutes | **Cooking time:** 20 minutes | **Servings:** 4

Ingredients:

- 4 chicken breasts, skinless and boneless
- 1 teaspoon chili powder
- 1 teaspoon olive oil
- 1 teaspoon ground paprika
- 1 teaspoon garlic powder
- 1 teaspoon minced garlic
- 1 tablespoon dill, chopped

Directions

1. Season chicken with all spices from pist above and sprinkle with olive oil.
2. After this, iput the chicken breasts in your air fryer's basket and cook at 350 degrees F for 10 minutes on each side.

Nutrition value/serving: calories 296, fat 12.2, fiber 0.6, carbs 1.8, protein 42.7

Green Chicken

Prep time: 10 minutes | **Cooking time:** 25 minutes | **Servings:** 4

Ingredients:

- 12 oz chicken fillets
- 1 teaspoon olive oil
- ½ teaspoon chili powder
- 4 teaspoons pesto sauce

Directions

1. In the shallow bowl mix up pesto sauce, chili powder, and olive oil.
2. Then rub the chicken fillets with the pesto mixture.
3. Preheat the air fryer to 390F. Put the chicken fillets in the air fryer basket and cook them for 25 minutes.

Nutritional value/serving: calories 195, fat 9.7, fiber 0.2, carbs 0.5, protein 25.1

Chicken and Vegetables Mix

Prep time: 5 minutes | **Cooking time:** 25 minutes | **Servings:** 4

Ingredients:

- 4 chicken breasts, skinless, boneless and halved
- 2 zucchinis, sliced
- 4 tomatoes, cut into wedges
- 2 green peppers, chopped
- 2 tablespoons sesame oil
- 1 teaspoon Italian seasoning

Directions

1. Pit all ingredients in the air fryer basket and mix well.
2. Cook the meal at 380 degrees F for 25 minutes. Divide everything between plates and serve.

Nutritional value/serving: calories 391, fat 18.5, fiber 3.6, carbs 9.8, protein 45

Cornish Chicken with Celery Stalk

Prep time: 20 minutes | **Cooking time:** 65 minutes | **Servings:** 4

Ingredients:

- 14 oz Cornish chicken
- 1 teaspoon lemongrass
- 1 oz celery stalk, chopped
- 2 tablespoons olive oil
- 2 tablespoons lemon juice
- ½ teaspoon lemon zest, grated
- 1 teaspoon salt
- 1 teaspoon chili powder
- ½ teaspoon ground black pepper

Directions

1. In the mixing bowl mix up lemongrass, lemon juice, lemon zest, salt, and ground black pepper.
2. Then add celery stalk.
3. After this, rub the Cornish chicken with the spice mixture and leave for 10 minutes to marinate.
4. Meanwhile, preheat the air fryer to 375F. Put the hen in the air fryer and cook it for 55 minutes. Then flip it on another side and cook for 10 minutes more.

Nutrition value/serving: calories 324, fat 25.3, fiber 0.5, carbs 1.1, protein 22.3

Cheese Chicken Balls

Prep time: 10 minutes | **Cooking time:** 12 minutes | Servings: 4

Ingredients:

- 12 oz ground chicken
- ½ cup almond flour
- 2 egg whites, whisked
- 1 teaspoon ground black pepper
- 1 egg yolk
- 1 teaspoon salt
- 4 oz Provolone cheese, grated
- 1 teaspoon ground coriander
- ½ teaspoon chili powder
- 1 tablespoon avocado oil

Directions

1. In the mixing bowl mix up ground chicken, ground black pepper, egg yolk, salt, Provolone cheese, ground coriander, and chili powder.
2. Stir the mixture until homogenous and make the small chicken balls.
3. Dip the chicken balls in the whisked egg whites and coat in the almond flour. Preheat the air fryer to 370F.
4. Put the chicken balls in the air fryer basket and cook them for 6 minutes from both sides.

Nutrition value/serving: calories 310, fat 17.3, fiber 0.8, carbs 2.4, protein 35.2

Thyme Chicken Thighs

Prep time: 5 minutes | **Cooking time:** 30 minutes | Servings: 4

Ingredients:

- 4 chicken thighs, bone-in and skinless
- 1 cup okra, chopped
- ½ cup coconut oil, melted
- Zest of 1 lime, grated
- 4 garlic cloves, minced
- 1 tablespoon thyme, chopped
- 1 tablespoon dill, chopped

Directions

1. Heat up a pan with half of the coconut oil over medium heat, add the chicken thighs and brown them for 2-3 minutes on each side.
2. Add the rest of the coconut oil, the okra and all the remaining ingredients, toss the meal.
3. Transfer it in the air fryer and cook at 370 degrees F for 20 minutes.

Nutrition value/serving: calories 531, fat 38.2, fiber 1.2, carbs 3.7, protein 43.1

Lime Chicken Drumsticks

Prep time: 10 minutes | **Cooking time:** 20 minutes | Servings: 3

Ingredients:

- 6 chicken drumsticks, skinless
- 1 teaspoon dried oregano
- 1 tablespoon lime juice
- ½ teaspoon lime zest, grated
- 1 teaspoon ground coriander
- ½ teaspoon chili powder
- 1 teaspoon garlic powder
- 1 tablespoon olive oil

Directions

1. Rub the chicken drumsticks with dried oregano, lime juice, lime zest, ground cumin, chili powder, garlic powder, and ground coriander.
2. Then sprinkle them with olive oil and put in the air fryer. Cook the chicken drumsticks for 20 minutes at 375F.

Nutrition value/serving: calories 202, fat 10.1, fiber 0.5, carbs 1.3, protein 25.6

Garlic Chicken Bites

Prep time: 5 minutes | **Cooking time:** 30 minutes | Servings: 4

Ingredients:

- 2 pounds chicken fillets, roughly chopped
- ¼ cup sesame oil
- Juice of 2 limes
- Zest of 1 lime, grated
- 2 garlic cloves, minced

Directions

1. In a bowl, mix the chopped chicken with the rest of the ingredients and toss well.
2. Put the chicken bites in your air fryer's basket and cook at 400 degrees F for 30 minutes, shaking halfway.

Nutrition value/serving: calories 559, fat 30.5, fiber 0.1, carbs 2.4, protein 65.8

Chicken Wings with Cream Cheese

Prep time: 15 minutes | **Cooking time:** 16 minutes | Servings: 4

Ingredients:

- 1-pound chicken wings, skinless
- ¼ cup cream cheese
- 1 tablespoon lemon juice
- ½ teaspoon smoked paprika
- ½ teaspoon ground coriander
- 1 teaspoon avocado oil

Directions

1. In the mixing bowl mix up cream cheese, lemon juice, smoked paprika, and ground coriander.
2. Then add the chicken wings and coat them in the cream cheese mixture well. Leave the chicken winds in the cream cheese mixture for 10-15 minutes to marinate.
3. Meanwhile, preheat the air fryer to 380F. Put the chicken wings in the air fryer and cook them for 8 minutes. Then flip the chicken wings on another and brush with cream cheese marinade.
4. Cook the chicken wings for 8 minutes more.

Nutrition value/serving: calories 269, fat 13.7, fiber 0.2, carbs 0.7, protein 34

Parmesan Chicken Wings

Prep time: 5 minutes | **Cooking time:** 30 minutes | **Servings:** 4

Ingredients:

- 2 pounds chicken wings, skinless
- ½ teaspoon ground white pepper
- 3 garlic cloves, minced
- 3 tablespoons coconut oil, melted
- ½ cup coconut cream
- ½ teaspoon basil, dried
- ½ teaspoon oregano, dried
- ¼ cup parmesan, grated

Directions

1. In a baking dish, mix the chicken wings with all the ingredients except the parmesan and toss.
2. Put the dish to your air fryer and cook at 380 degrees F for 30 minutes.
3. Sprinkle the meal with cheese, leave the mix aside for 10 minutes.

Nutrition value/serving: calories 598, fat 34.6, fiber 0.9, carbs 2.8, protein 67.1

Parsley Chicken

Prep time: 15 minutes | **Cooking time:** 20 minutes | **Servings:** 6

Ingredients:

- 18 oz chicken breast, skinless, boneless
- 3 oz Parmesan, grated
- 3 eggs, beaten
- 1 teaspoon chili powder
- 1 teaspoon ground paprika
- 2 tablespoons sesame oil
- 1 teaspoon Erythritol
- ¼ teaspoon garlic powder
- 1 teaspoon cayenne pepper
- ½ teaspoon dried parsley

Directions

1. In the shallow bowl mix up chili powder, ground paprika, Erythritol, garlic powder, and cayenne pepper. Add dried parsley and stir the mixture gently.
2. Then rub the chicken breast in the spice mixture. Dip the chicken breast in the beaten eggs.
3. After this, coat it in the Parmesan and dip in the eggs again. Then sprinkle with sesame oil.
4. Preheat the air fryer to 380F. Put the chicken breast in the air fryer and cook it for 16 minutes. Then flip the chicken breast on another side and cook it for 4 minutes more.

Nutrition value/serving: calories 217, fat 12.1, fiber 0.4, carbs 1.3, protein 25.5

Coconut Aminos Chicken

Prep time: 5 minutes | **Cooking time:** 20 minutes | **Servings:** 4

Ingredients:

- 4 chicken breasts, skinless, boneless and halved
- 4 tablespoons coconut aminos
- 1 teaspoon coconut oil
- ¼ cup water
- 1 tablespoon ginger, grated

Directions

1. Combine the chicken with the ginger and all the ingredients and toss.
2. Put the mixture in your air fryer and cook at 380 degrees F for 20, shaking the fryer halfway.

Nutrition value/serving: calories 307, fat 12, fiber 0.2, carbs 4, protein 42.4

Tomato and Garlic Chicken

Prep time: 10 minutes | **Cooking time:** 18 minutes | **Servings:** 4

Ingredients:

- 1-pound chicken breast, skinless, boneless
- 1 tablespoon keto tomato sauce
- 1 teaspoon olive oil
- ½ teaspoon garlic, minced
- 1 teaspoon lemon juice

Directions

1. In the small bowl mix up tomato sauce, olive oil, and garlic.
2. Then brush the chicken breast with the tomato sauce mixture well.
3. Preheat the air fryer to 385F. Place the chicken breast in the air fryer and cook it for 15 minutes. Then flip it on another side and cook for 3 minutes more. Slice the cooked chicken breast into servings.

Nutrition value/serving: calories 140, fat 4, fiber 0, carbs 0.2, protein 24.1

Chicken and Zucchini Bowl

Prep time: 15 minutes | **Cooking time:** 25 minutes | **Servings:** 2

Ingredients:

- 1 pound chicken thighs, boneless and skinless
- Juice of 1 lime
- 2 tablespoons avocado oil
- 1 teaspoon dried garlic
- 1 teaspoon basil, dried
- 1 zucchinis, halved lengthwise and sliced into half-moons

Directions

1. In a bowl, mix the chicken with all the ingredients except the zucchinis, toss and leave aside for 15 minutes.
2. Add the zucchinis toss, put everything into a pan that fits the air fryer, and cook at 380 degrees F for 25 minutes.
3. Divide everything between plates and serve.

Nutrition value/serving: calories 467, fat 18.8, fiber 1.7, carbs 4.5, protein 67.1

Ghee Chicken

Prep time: 15 minutes | **Cooking time:** 30 minutes | **Servings:** 4

Ingredients:

- 12 oz chicken fillet, chopped
- 1 teaspoon chili flakes
- ½ teaspoon ground cumin
- ½ teaspoon garlic powder
- 1 teaspoon ground turmeric
- ½ teaspoon ground paprika
- ¼ cup almond flour
- 3 tablespoon ghee, melted

Directions

1. In the mixing bowl mix up chili flakes, ground cumin, garlic powder, ground turmeric, ground paprika, and almond flour.
2. Then mix chicken with ghee and coat well in the almond flour mixture.
3. Preheat the air fryer to 380F. Place the chicken in the air fryer in one layer.
4. Cook the meal for 15 minutes. Then flip the chicken legs on another side and cook them for 15 minutes more.

Nutrition value/serving: calories 261, fat 16.9, fiber 0.5, carbs 1.3, protein 25.2

Nutmeg Chicken

Prep time: 15 minutes | **Cooking time:** 12 minutes | **Servings:** 4

Ingredients:

- 12 oz chicken fillet (3 oz each fillet)
- 4 teaspoons coconut shred
- 1 egg white, whisked
- 1 teaspoon ground nutmeg

Directions

1. Beat the chicken fillets with the kitchen hammer.
2. Then dip every chicken chop in the whisked egg white nutmeg, and coat in the coconut shred.
3. Preheat the air fryer to 360F. Put the chicken chops in the air fryer and spray with cooking spray. Cook the chicken chop for 7 minutes. Then flip them on another side and cook for 5 minutes.
4. The cooked chicken chops should have a golden brown color.

Nutrition value/serving: calories 182, fat 7.3, fiber 0.3, carbs 1.7, protein 25.7

Greece Style Chicken

Prep time: 10 minutes | **Cooking time:** 30 minutes | **Servings:** 4

Ingredients:

- 8 chicken thighs, boneless and skinless
- 2 tablespoons avocado oil
- 1 teaspoon oregano, dried
- ½ teaspoon garlic powder
- ½ cup green olives, chopped, pitted
- ½ cup kalamata olives, pitted and sliced
- ¼ cup parmesan, grated

Directions

1. Heat up a pan that fits the air fryer with the oil over medium-high heat, add the chicken and brown for 2 minutes on each side.
2. Add all the other ingredients except the parmesan and toss.
3. Put the pan in the air fryer, sprinkle the parmesan on top and cook at 370 degrees F for 25 minutes.

Nutrition value/serving: calories 592, fat 24.7, fiber 1, carbs 1.9, protein 85.3

Lime and Basil Chicken

Prep time: 10 minutes | **Cooking time:** 25 minutes | **Servings:** 4

Ingredients:

- ½ cup basil, minced
- 2 tablespoons avocado oil
- 1 tablespoon lime juice

- 1 ½ pounds chicken wings, skinless

Directions

1. In a bowl, mix the chicken wings with all the ingredients and toss well.
2. Put the chicken wings in the air fryer's basket and cook at 380 degrees F for 25 minutes.

Nutrition value/serving: calories 333, fat 13.5, fiber 0.4, carbs 0.5, protein 49.4

Smoked Paprika Chicken Wings

Prep time: 5 minutes | **Cooking time:** 30 minutes | **Servings:** 4

Ingredients:

- 1 tablespoon avocado oil
- 2 pounds chicken wings, skinless
- 1 tablespoon lemon juice
- 2 teaspoons smoked paprika

Directions

1. In a bowl, mix the chicken wings with all the other ingredients and toss well.
2. Put the chicken wings in your air fryer's basket and cook at 380 degrees F for 15 minutes on each side.

Nutrition value/serving: calories 440, fat 17.4, fiber 0.6, carbs 0.9, protein 65.8

Keto Hoisin Chicken

Prep time: 25 minutes | **Cooking time:** 22 minutes | **Servings:** 2

Ingredients:

- ½ teaspoon keto hoisin sauce
- ½ teaspoon ground black pepper
- ½ teaspoon ground cumin
- ¼ teaspoon xanthan gum
- 1 teaspoon apple cider vinegar
- 1 tablespoon avocado oil
- 3 tablespoons organic almond milk
- ½ teaspoon minced garlic
- ½ teaspoon chili paste
- 1-pound chicken drumsticks, skinless

Directions

1. Mix the chicken drumsticks with hoison sauce, ground black pepper, cumin, xanthan gum, apple cider vinegar, avocado oil, and almond milk.
2. Then add chili paste and minced garlic.
3. Leave to marinate for 10 minutes more.
4. Preheat the air fryer to 375F. Put the chicken drumsticks in the air fryer and cook them for 22 minutes.

Nutrition value/serving: calories 460, fat 19.6, fiber 2.7, carbs 4.6, protein 63.3

Chicken Mix

Prep time: 5 minutes | **Cooking time:** 25 minutes | **Servings:** 4

Ingredients:

- 4 chicken thighs, skinless, boneless
- 1 tablespoon avocado oil
- 1 tablespoon thyme, chopped
- 1 cup water
- 3 garlic cloves, minced
- ½ cup coconut cream
- 1 cup sun-dried tomatoes, chopped
- 4 tablespoons parmesan, grated

Directions

1. Heat up a pan with the oil over medium-high heat, add the chicken, and garlic, and brown for 2-3 minutes on each side. Add the rest of the ingredients except the parmesan, toss, put the pan in the air fryer and cook at 370 degrees F for 20 minutes.
2. Sprinkle the parmesan on top, leave the mix aside for 5 minutes.

Nutrition value/serving: calories 364, fat 18.6, fiber 1.7, carbs 4.8, protein 43.6

Stuffed Chicken with Cheese

Prep time: 20 minutes | **Cooking time:** 25 minutes | **Servings:** 3

Ingredients:

- 1 ½-pound chicken breast, skinless, boneless
- ½ cup broccoli, shredded
- 1 jalapeno pepper, chopped
- ¼ cup Cheddar cheese, shredded
- ½ teaspoon cayenne pepper
- 1 tablespoon avocado oil
- ½ teaspoon dried thyme

Directions

1. Make the horizontal cut in the chicken breast. In the mixing bowl mix up shredded broccoli, chopped jalapeno pepper, and cayenne pepper. Fill the chicken cut with the shredded broccoli and secure the cut with toothpicks.
2. Then sprinkle the chicken breast with cheese, dried thyme, and avocado oil.
3. Preheat the air fryer to 380F. Put the chicken breast in the air fryer and cook it for 20 minutes.

Nutrition value/serving: calories 311, fat 9.5, fiber 0.9, carbs 2, protein 51

Chicken with Lime Sauce

Prep time: 5 minutes | **Cooking time:** 25 minutes | Servings: 4

Ingredients:

- ¼ white onion, chopped
- 1 tablespoon ginger, grated
- 4 garlic cloves, minced
- 2 tablespoons coconut aminos
- 8 chicken drumsticks
- ½ cup water
- 1 teaspoon olive oil
- ¼ cup cilantro, chopped
- 1 tablespoon lime juice

Directions

1. Heat up a pan with the oil over medium-high heat, add the chicken drumsticks, brown them for 2 minutes on each side and transfer to a pan that fits the fryer.
2. Add all the other ingredients, toss everything, put the pan in the fryer and cook at 370 degrees F for 20 minutes.
3. Divide the chicken and lime sauce (gravy) between plates and serve.

Nutrition value/serving: calories 185, fat 6.5, fiber 0.4, carbs 4.1, protein 25.7

Keto Chicken Quesadilla

Prep time: 15 minutes | **Cooking time:** 10 minutes | Servings: 2

Ingredients:

- 2 low carb tortillas
- 7 oz chicken breast, skinless, boneless, boiled
- 1 tablespoon cream cheese
- 1 teaspoon coconut oil, melted
- 1 teaspoon minced garlic
- 1 teaspoon fresh parsley, chopped
- ½ teaspoon salt
- 2 oz Monterey Jack cheese, shredded

Directions

1. Shred the chicken breast with the help of the fork and put it in the bowl. Add cream cheese, coconut oil, minced garlic, parsley, and salt.
2. Add shredded Monterey jack cheese and stir the shredded chicken. T
3. Then put 1 tortilla in the air fryer baking pan. Top it with the shredded chicken mixture and cover with the second corn tortilla.
4. Cook the meal for 5 minutes at 400F.

Nutrition value/serving: calories 338, fat 17.1, fiber 7.1, carbs 12.8, protein 31.5

Chicken and Spinach

Prep time: 5 minutes | **Cooking time:** 24 minutes | Servings: 6

Ingredients:

- 6 chicken breasts, skinless, boneless and halved
- 2 tablespoons avocado oil
- 1 pound Cheddar cheese, sliced
- 2 cups baby spinach
- 1 tomato, sliced
- 1 tablespoon basil, chopped

Directions

1. Make slits in each chicken breast halves, and stuff with Cheddar cheese, spinach and tomatoes. Drizzle the oil over stuffed chicken, put it in your air fryer's basket and cook at 370 degrees F for 12 minutes on each side.
2. Divide between plates.

Nutrition value/serving: calories 593, fat 36.5, fiber 0.6, carbs 2, protein 61.5

Fragrant Turkey Bacon

Prep time: 10 minutes | **Cooking time:** 8 minutes | Servings: 2

Ingredients:

- 7 oz turkey bacon
- 1 teaspoon coconut oil, melted
- ½ teaspoon ground ginger

Directions

1. Slice the turkey bacon if needed and sprinkle it with ground ginger and coconut oil.
2. Preheat the air fryer to 400F. Arrange the turkey bacon in the air fryer in one layer and cook it for 4 minutes.
3. Then flip the bacon on another side and cook for 4 minutes more.

Nutrition value/serving: calories 149, fat 5.5, fiber 0.1, carbs 0.3, protein 19.3

Coriander Duck

Prep time: 5 minutes | **Cooking time:** 28 minutes | Servings: 6

Ingredients:

- 3 pounds duck fillet
- 1 teaspoon avocado oil
- ½ teaspoon salt
- ½ teaspoon ground coriander

Directions

1. Preheat the air fryer to 375F. Then sprinkle the duck with avocado oil, salt, and ground coriander.
2. Put the duck fillet in the air fryer and cook it for 18

minutes.

3. Then flip it on another side and cook for 10 minutes more.

Nutrition value/serving: calories 344, fat 7, fiber 0, carbs 0, protein 65.7

Almond Chicken Tenders

Prep time: 5 minutes | **Cooking time:** 20 minutes | **Servings:** 4

Ingredients:

- 4 chicken breasts, skinless, boneless and cut into tenders
- ½ teaspoon salt
- 1/3 cup almond flour
- 2 eggs, whisked
- 1/3 cup organic almond milk
- 9 ounces coconut flakes

Directions

1. Season the chicken tenders with salt and dredge them in almond flour, then dip in eggs and almond milk and sprinkle with coconut flakes.
2. Put the chicken tenders in your air fryer's basket and cook at 400 degrees F for 10 minutes on each side.

Nutrition value/serving: calories 594, fat 40.3, fiber 6.4, carbs 11.5, protein 48.1

Hot Cutlets

Prep time: 20 minutes | **Cooking time:** 16 minutes | **Servings:** 4

Ingredients:

- 15 oz chicken fillet
- 1 teaspoon chili powder
- 1 teaspoon ghee, melted
- ½ teaspoon garlic powder
- ¼ teaspoon chili flakes

Directions

1. Chop the chicken fillet into the tiny pieces. Then sprinkle the chopped chicken with garlic and chili powder.
2. Stir the mixture until homogenous. Make the medium-size cutlets from the mixture. Preheat the air fryer to 365F. Brush the air fryer basket with ghee and put the chicken cutlets inside.
3. Sprinkle the chicken cutlets with chili flakes.
4. Cook them for 8 minutes and then flip on another side with the help of the spatula.

Nutrition value/serving: calories 215, fat 9.1, fiber 0.3, carbs 0.6, protein 30.9

FISH AND SEAFOOD

Fish and Seafood

Scallops in Bacon Covering

Prep time: 15 minutes | **Cooking time:** 7 minutes | Servings: 4

Ingredients:

- 1 teaspoon dried thyme
- ½ teaspoon ground paprika
- ¼ teaspoon salt
- 16 oz scallops
- 4 oz bacon, sliced
- 1 teaspoon avocado oil

Directions

1. Sprinkle the scallops with dried thyme, ground paprika, and salt.
2. Then wrap the scallops in the bacon slices and secure with toothpicks.
3. Sprinkle the scallops with avocado oil.
4. Preheat the air fryer to 400F.
5. Put the scallops in the air fryer basket and cook them for 7 minutes.

Nutrition value/serving: calories 256, fat 12.9, fiber 0.2, carbs 3.5, protein 29.6

Salmon with Delicious Crust

Prep time: 15 minutes | **Cooking time:** 8 minutes | Servings: 4

Ingredients:

- 12 oz salmon fillet
- ¼ cup pistachios, grinded
- ½ teaspoon ground nutmeg
- 2 tablespoons almond flour
- ½ teaspoon ground turmeric
- ¼ teaspoon sage
- ½ teaspoon salt
- 1 tablespoon coconut cream
- Cooking spray

Directions

1. Cut the salmon fillet on 4 servings.
2. In the mixing bowl mix up ground turmeric, sage, salt, and coconut cream.
3. Then in the separated bowl mix up almond flour and pistachios.
4. Dip the salmon fillets in the coconut cream mixture and then coat in the pistachio mixture.
5. Preheat the air fryer to 380F.
6. Place the coated salmon fillets in the air fryer and spray them with the cooking spray.
7. Cook the fish for 8 minutes.

Nutrition value/serving: calories 224, fat 15, fiber 2.1, carbs 4.6, protein 20.4

Catfish Bites

Prep time: 10 minutes | **Cooking time:** 12 minutes | Servings: 4

Ingredients:

- 20 oz catfish fillet (4 oz each fillet)
- 2 eggs, beaten
- 1 teaspoon ground coriander
- ½ teaspoon salt
- 1 teaspoon lemon juice
- 1 teaspoon olive oil
- ¼ teaspoon cayenne pepper
- 1/3 cup coconut flour

Directions

1. Sprinkle the catfish fillets with ground coriander, salt, lemon juice cayenne pepper, and coconut flour.
2. Then sprinkle the fish fillets with olive oil.
3. Preheat the air fryer to 385F.
4. Put the catfish fillets in the air fryer basket and cook them for 8 minutes.
5. Then flip the fish on another side and cook for 4 minutes more.

Nutrition value/serving: calories 238, fat 14.3, fiber 0.5, carbs 0.9, protein 25

Haddock Fillets

Prep time: 10 minutes | **Cooking time:** 8 minutes | Servings: 4

Ingredients:

- 12 oz haddock fillet
- 1 egg, beaten
- 1 teaspoon coconut cream
- 1 teaspoon chili powder
- ½ teaspoon salt
- 1 tablespoon almond flour
- Cooking spray

Directions

1. Cut the haddock on 4 fillets and sprinkle with chili powder and salt.
2. After this, in the small bowl mix up egg, almond flour and coconut cream.
3. Dip the haddock pieces in the egg mixture and generously sprinkle with flax meal.
4. Preheat the air fryer to 400F.
5. Put the prepared haddock pieces in the air fryer in one layer and cook them for 4 minutes from each side or until they are golden brown.

Nutrition value/serving: calories 126, fat 3.2, fiber 0.4, carbs 0.9, protein 22.5

Garlic and Cumin Shrimps

Prep time: 10 minutes | **Cooking time:** 5 minutes | **Servings:** 3

Ingredients:

- 1-pound shrimps, peeled
- ½ teaspoon dried basil
- ¼ teaspoon minced garlic
- 1 teaspoon ground cumin
- ¼ teaspoon lime zest, grated
- ½ tablespoon sesame oil
- ½ teaspoon dried parsley

Directions

1. In the mixing bowl mix up shrimps, minced garlic, ground cumin, lime zest, and dried parsley.
2. Then add sesame oil and mix up the shrimps well.
3. Preheat the air fryer to 400F.
4. Put the shrimps in the preheated air fryer basket and cook for 5 minutes.

Nutrition value/serving: calories 203, fat 5, fiber 0.1, carbs 2.7, protein 34.6

Blackened Tilapia

Prep time: 10 minutes | **Cooking time:** 8 minutes | **Servings:** 2

Ingredients:

- 10 oz tilapia fillet
- ½ teaspoon cayenne pepper
- ¼ teaspoon ground coriander
- ½ teaspoon ground ginger
- 1 tablespoon olive oil
- ½ teaspoon salt
- ½ teaspoon dried rosemary
- ½ teaspoon ground paprika

Directions

1. In the shallow bowl mix up cayenne pepper, ground coriander, ginger, salt, dried rosemary, and ground paprika.
2. Then rub the tilapia fillet with the spice mixture.
3. After this, sprinkle it with olive oil.
4. Preheat the air fryer to 390F.
5. Place the tilapia fillet in the air fryer and cook it for 4 minutes.
6. Then carefully flip the fish on another side and cook for 4 minutes more.

Nutrition value/serving: calories 182, fat 8.5, fiber 0.5, carbs 1.1, protein 26.6

Tender Shrimp Skewers

Prep time: 10 minutes | **Cooking time:** 5 minutes | **Servings:** 5

Ingredients:

- 4-pounds shrimps, peeled
- 2 tablespoons fresh parsley, chopped
- 2 tablespoons apple cider vinegar
- 1 tablespoon sesame oil
- Cooking spray

Directions

1. In the shallow bowl mix up sesame oil, apple cider vinegar, and fresh parsley.
2. Then put the shrimps in the big bowl and sprinkle with sesame oil mixture.
3. Mix them well and leave for 10 minutes to marinate.
4. After this, string the shrimps on the skewers.
5. Preheat the air fryer to 400F.
6. Arrange the shrimp skewers in the air fryer and cook them for 5 minutes.

Nutrition value/serving: calories 457, fat 8.9, fiber 0.1, carbs 5.7, protein 82.7

Crab and Egg Muffins

Prep time: 15 minutes | **Cooking time:** 20 minutes | **Servings:** 2

Ingredients:

- 5 oz crab meat, chopped
- 2 eggs, beaten
- 2 tablespoons coconut flour
- ¼ teaspoon baking powder
- ½ teaspoon lemon juice
- ½ teaspoon ground paprika
- 1 tablespoon coconut oil, softened
- Cooking spray

Directions

1. Grind the chopped crab meat and put it in the bowl.
2. Add eggs, coconut flour, baking powder, lemon juice, ground paprika, and coconut oil.
3. Stir the mixture until homogenous.
4. Preheat the air fryer to 365F.
5. Spray the muffin molds with cooking spray.
6. Then pour the crab meat batter in the muffin molds and place them in the preheated air fryer.
7. Cook the crab muffins for 20 minutes or until they are light brown.
8. Cool the cooked muffins to the room temperature and remove from the muffin mold.

Nutrition value/serving: calories 247, fat 14.5, fiber 5.2, carbs 10.2, protein 16.5

Stuffed Mackerel

Prep time: 15 minutes | **Cooking time:** 20 minutes | Servings: 2

Ingredients:

- 1-pound mackerel, trimmed
- 1 tablespoon ground coriander
- 1 red bell pepper
- ½ white onion, sliced
- 1 tablespoon olive oil
- 1 teaspoon lime juice
- ½ teaspoon salt

Directions

1. Wash the mackerel if needed and sprinkle with ground coriander
2. Chop the red bell pepper.
3. Then fill the mackerel with bell pepper and white onion.
4. After this, sprinkle the fish with olive oil, lime juice, and salt.
5. Preheat the air fryer to 375F.
6. Place the mackerel in the air fryer basket and cook it for 20 minutes.

Nutrition value/serving: calories 690, fat 47.6, fiber 1.5, carbs 8.9, protein 55.1

Sardine Cakes

Prep time: 15 minutes | **Cooking time:** 10 minutes | Servings: 4

Ingredients:

- 12 oz sardines, trimmed, cleaned
- ¼ cup almond flour
- 1 egg, beaten
- 2 tablespoons flax meal
- 1 teaspoon ground paprika
- 1 teaspoon salt
- Cooking spray

Directions

1. Chop the sardines roughly and put them in the bowl.
2. Add almond flour, egg, flax meal, ground paprika, and salt.
3. Mix up the mixture with the help of the fork.
4. Then make 5 cakes from the sardine mixture.
5. Preheat the air fryer to 390F.
6. Spray the air fryer basket with cooking spray and place the cakes inside.
7. Cook them for 5 minutes from each side.

Nutrition value/serving: calories 251, fat 15.5, fiber 2, carbs 2.9, protein 24.7

Salmon Bites

Prep time: 15 minutes | **Cooking time:** 10 minutes | Servings: 4

Ingredients:

- 24 oz salmon steaks (6 oz each fillet)
- ½ teaspoon salt
- ½ teaspoon ground white pepper
- 4 oz bacon, sliced
- 1 tablespoon olive oil

Directions

1. Cut every salmon fillet on 2 parts and sprinkle with salt and ground white pepper.
2. Then wrap the fish fillets in the sliced bacon.
3. Preheat the air fryer to 400F.
4. Sprinkle the halibut bites with olive oil and put in the air fryer basket.
5. Cook the meal for 5 minutes.
6. Then flip the fish bites on another side and cook them for 5 minutes more.

Nutrition value/serving: calories 409, fat 25.9, fiber 0.1, carbs 0.6, protein 43.5

Cheesy Shrimps

Prep time: 15 minutes | **Cooking time:** 5 minutes | Servings: 4

Ingredients:

- 14 oz shrimps, peeled
- 2 eggs, beaten
- ¼ cup coconut cream
- 1 teaspoon salt
- 1 teaspoon ground black pepper
- 4 oz Cheddar cheese, shredded
- 5 tablespoons almond flour
- 1 tablespoon lemon juice, for garnish

Directions

1. In the mixing bowl mix up coconut cream, salt, and ground black pepper.
2. Add eggs and whisk the mixture until homogenous.
3. After this, mix up almond flour and Cheddar cheese.
4. Dip the shrimps in the coconut cream mixture and coat in the almond flour mixture.
5. Then dip the shrimps in the egg mixture again and coat in the coconut flour.
6. Preheat the air fryer to 400F.
7. Arrange the shrimps in the air fryer in one layer and cook them for 5 minutes.
8. Repeat the same step with remaining shrimps.
9. Sprinkle the bang-bang shrimps with lemon juice.

Nutrition value/serving: calories 350, fat 21.3, fiber 1.4, carbs 5.2, protein 34.7

Catfish in Coat

Prep time: 10 minutes | **Cooking time:** 10 minutes | **Servings:** 2

Ingredients:

- ¼ cup coconut flakes
- 3 tablespoons almond flour
- 1 teaspoon salt
- 1 teaspoon ground paprika
- 3 eggs, beaten
- 10 oz catfish fillet
- Cooking spray

Directions

1. Cut the catfish fillet on the medium pieces and sprinkle with salt and ground paprika.
2. After this, dip the catfish pieces in the egg and coat in the almond flour.
3. Then dip the fish pieces in the egg again and coat in the coconut flakes.
4. Preheat the air fryer to 385F.
5. Place the catfish pieces in the air fryer basket and cook them for 6 minutes.
6. Then flip the fish on another side and cook them for 4 minutes more.

Nutrition value/serving: calories 390, fat 26.1, fiber 2.4, carbs 4.9, protein 33.1

Turmeric Fish Fillets

Prep time: 10 minutes | **Cooking time:** 7 minutes | **Servings:** 2

Ingredients:

- 8 oz salmon fillet
- 2 tablespoons coconut flakes
- 1 tablespoon organic almond milk
- ½ teaspoon salt
- ½ teaspoon ground turmeric
- ½ teaspoon garlic powder
- 1 teaspoon olive oil

Directions

1. Cut the salmon fillet into halves and sprinkle with salt, ground turmeric, and garlic powder.
2. After this, dip the fish fillets in the almond milk and coat in the coconut flakes.
3. Sprinkle the salmon fillets with olive oil.
4. Preheat the air fryer to 380F.
5. Arrange the salmon fillets in the air fryer basket and cook for 7 minutes.

Nutrition value/serving: calories 209, fat 12.9, fiber 0.8, carbs 2.1, protein 22.5

Onion and Tilapia

Prep time: 15 minutes | **Cooking time:** 9 minutes | **Servings:** 2

Ingredients:

- 1 white onion, chopped
- 1 teaspoon chili flakes
- 1 tablespoon olive oil
- ½ teaspoon salt
- 10 oz tilapia fillet

Directions

1. In the shallow bowl mix up onion, chili flakes, salt.
2. Gently churn the mixture and add olive oil.
3. After this, slice the tilapia fillet and sprinkle with chili mixture.
4. Massage the fish with the help of the fingertips gently and leave for 10 minutes to marinate.
5. Preheat the air fryer to 390F.
6. Put the tilapia fillets in the air fryer basket and cook for 5 minutes.
7. Then flip the fish on another side and cook for 4 minutes more.

Nutrition value/serving: calories 199, fat 8.3, fiber 1.2, carbs 5.2, protein 27

Sweet Salmon Fillet

Prep time: 10 minutes | **Cooking time:** 9 minutes | **Servings:** 6

Ingredients:

- 18 oz salmon fillet
- 2 tablespoons Erythritol
- 1 tablespoon lemon juice
- 6 teaspoons liquid aminos
- 1 teaspoon minced ginger
- 1 tablespoon sesame seeds
- 2 tablespoons lime juice
- ½ teaspoon minced garlic
- 1 tablespoon olive oil

Directions

1. Cut the salmon fillet on 8 servings and sprinkle with lemon juice, minced ginger, lime juice, minced garlic, a liquid aminos.
2. Leave the fish for 10-15 minutes to marinate.
3. After this, sprinkle the fish with olive oil and put in the preheated to 380F air fryer in one layer.
4. Cook the fish fillets for 7 minutes.
5. Then sprinkle them with Erythritol and sesame seeds and cook for 2 minutes more at 400F.

Nutrition value/serving: calories 143, fat 8.4, fiber 0.2, carbs 0.9, protein 17.5

Ginger Mussels

Prep time: 10 minutes | **Cooking time:** 2 minutes | Servings: 5

Ingredients:

- 2-pounds mussels
- 1 shallot, chopped
- 1 tablespoon fresh ginger, minced
- 1 tablespoon coconut, melted
- 1 teaspoon sunflower oil
- 1 teaspoon salt
- 1 tablespoon fresh parsley, chopped
- ½ teaspoon chili flakes

Directions

1. Clean and wash mussels and put them in the big bowl.
2. Add shallot, minced ginger, coconut oil, sunflower oil, salt, and chili flakes.
3. Shake the mussels well.
4. Preheat the air fryer to 390F.
5. Put the mussels in the air fryer basket and cook for 2 minutes.
6. Then transfer the cooked meal in the serving bowl and top it with chopped fresh parsley.

Nutrition value/serving: calories 173, fat 5.4, fiber 0.3, carbs 8, protein 21.8

Salmon Canoes

Prep time: 10 minutes | **Cooking time:** 9 minutes | Servings: 2

Ingredients:

- 1-pound salmon
- 1 tablespoon swerve
- 1 tablespoon butter, melted
- ½ teaspoon cayenne pepper
- 1 teaspoon water
- ¼ teaspoon ground nutmeg

Directions

1. In the small bowl mix up swerve and water.
2. Then rub the salmon with ground nutmeg and cayenne pepper.
3. After this, brush the fish with swerve liquid and sprinkle with melted butter.
4. Put the salmon on the foil. Make the shape of Canoes.
5. Preheat the air fryer to 385F.
6. Transfer the salmon canoes in the air fryer basket and cook for 9 minutes.

Nutrition value/serving: calories 354, fat 19.9, fiber 0.2, carbs 0.4, protein 44.1

Tender Lobster Tail

Prep time: 10 minutes | **Cooking time:** 6 minutes | Servings: 4

Ingredients:

- 4 lobster tails, peeled
- 4 teaspoons butter
- ½ teaspoon salt
- ½ teaspoon dried basil

Directions

1. Make the cut on the back of every lobster tail and sprinkle them with dried basil and salt.
2. Preheat the air fryer to 380F.
3. Place the lobster tails in the air fryer basket and cook them for 5 minutes.
4. After this, gently spread the lobster tails with butter and cook for 1 minute more.

Nutrition value/serving: calories 114, fat 4.3, fiber 0, carbs 1, protein 17

Fish Sticks

Prep time: 15 minutes | **Cooking time:** 9 minutes | Servings: 2

Ingredients:

- 1-pound haddock fillet
- ½ cup almond flour
- 2 eggs, beaten
- ½ teaspoon ground coriander
- 1 tablespoon flax meal
- 1 teaspoon salt
- 1 teaspoon olive oil

Directions

1. Slice the haddock fillets into the strips.
2. In the mixing bowl, mix up eggs, ground coriander, and salt. Stir the liquid until salt is dissolved.
3. Then in the separated bowl mix up almond flour and flax meal.
4. Dip the haddock sticks in the egg mixture and coat in the almond flour mixture.
5. Preheat the air fryer to 400F.
6. Place the fish sticks in the air fryer basket in one layer and sprinkle with olive oil.
7. Cook the fish sticks for 4 minutes.
8. Then flip them on another side and cook for 5 minutes more or until the fish sticks are golden brown.

Nutrition value/serving: calories 512, fat 24.1, fiber 4, carbs 7.3, protein 67.3

Rosemary Salmon

Prep time: 10 minutes | **Cooking time:** 15 minutes | Servings: 2

Ingredients:

- 1 teaspoon dried rosemary
- ½ teaspoon dried basil
- ½ teaspoon ground paprika
- ½ teaspoon salt
- 1-pound salmon
- 1 tablespoon avocado oil

Directions

1. In the bowl mix up spices: dried rosemary, basil, paprika, and salt.
2. After this, gently rub the salmon with the spice mixture and sprinkle with avocado oil.
3. Preheat the air fryer to 375F.
4. Line the air fryer with baking paper and put the prepared salmon inside.
5. Cook the fish for 15 minutes or until you get the light crunchy crust.

Nutrition value/serving: calories 313, fat 15.1, fiber 0.8, carbs 1.1, protein 44.2

Nutmeg Tuna Boats

Prep time: 15 minutes | **Cooking time:** 12 minutes | Servings: 2

Ingredients:

- 1 avocado, pitted, halved
- 6 oz tuna, canned
- 1 egg, beaten
- ½ teaspoon salt
- ½ teaspoon ground paprika
- ½ teaspoon ground nutmeg
- 1 teaspoon dried dill
- Cooking spray

Directions

1. Scoop ½ part of the avocado meat from the avocado to get the avocado boats. Use the scooper for this step.
2. After this, in the mixing bowl mix up tuna and egg. Shred the mixture with the help of the fork.
3. Add salt, paprika ground nutmeg, and dried dill. Stir the tuna mixture until homogenous.
4. Add the scooped avocado meat and mix up the mixture well.
5. Fill the avocado boats with tuna mixture.
6. Preheat the air fryer to 385F.
7. Arrange the tuna boats in the air fryer basket and cook them for 12 minutes.

Nutrition value/serving: calories 400, fat 29, fiber 7.1, carbs 9.7, protein 27.5

Thyme Scallops

Prep time: 15 minutes | **Cooking time:** 6 minutes | Servings: 3

Ingredients:

- 12 oz scallops
- 1 tablespoon dried thyme
- ½ teaspoon salt
- 1 tablespoon butter, melted

Directions

1. Mix up salt, butter, and dried thyme.
2. Brush the scallops with thyme mixture and leave for 5 minutes to marinate.
3. Meanwhile, preheat the air fryer to 400F.
4. Put the marinated scallops in the air fryer and sprinkle them with remaining butter and thyme mixture.
5. Cook the scallops for 4 minutes.
6. Then flip them on another side and cook for 2 minutes more.

Nutrition value/serving: calories 136, fat 4.8, fiber 0.3, carbs 3.3, protein 19.2

Calamari in Coconut Flakes

Prep time: 10 minutes | **Cooking time:** 6 minutes | Servings: 2

Ingredients:

- 6 oz calamari, trimmed
- 2 tablespoons coconut flakes
- 1 egg, beaten
- 1 teaspoon ground cumin
- ½ teaspoon salt
- Cooking spray

Directions

1. Slice the calamari into the rings and sprinkle them with cumin and salt.
2. Then transfer the calamari rings in the bowl with a beaten egg and stir them gently.
3. After this, sprinkle the calamari rings with coconut flakes and shake well.
4. Preheat the air fryer to 400F.
5. Put the calamari rings in the air fryer basket and spray them with cooking spray.
6. Cook the meal for 3 minutes.
7. Then gently stir the calamari and cook them for 3 minutes more.

Nutrition value/serving: calories 267, fat 12.1, fiber 1.6 carbs 8.4, protein 19.1

Cod and Chives Cakes

Prep time: 15 minutes | **Cooking time:** 12 minutes | **Servings:** 2

Ingredients:

- ½ cup broccoli, shredded
- 4 oz cod fillet, chopped
- 1 egg, beaten
- 1 teaspoon chives, chopped
- ¼ teaspoon ground paprika
- 1 teaspoon salt
- ½ teaspoon ground cumin
- 2 tablespoons almond flour
- 1 tablespoon onion, minced
- 1 tablespoon sesame oil

Directions

1. Grind the chopped cod fillet and put it in the mixing bowl.
2. Add shredded broccoli, egg, chives, ground paprika, salt, ground cumin, and minced onion.
3. Stir the mixture until homogenous and add almond flour.
4. Stir it again.
5. After this, make the medium size cakes.
6. Preheat the air fryer to 385F.
7. Place the cakes in the air fryer basket and sprinkle with sesame oil.
8. Cook the fish cakes for 8 minutes.
9. Then flip them on another side and cook for 4 minutes more or until the cakes are light brown.

Nutrition value/serving: calories 310, fat 23.7, fiber 3.9, carbs 8.5, protein 19.7

Basil Crawfish

Prep time: 10 minutes | **Cooking time:** 5 minutes | **Servings:** 2

Ingredients:

- 1-pound crawfish
- 1 tablespoon olive oil
- 1 teaspoon onion powder
- 1 tablespoon basil, chopped

Directions

1. Preheat the air fryer to 340F.
2. Place the crawfish in the air fryer basket and sprinkle with olive oil and basil.
3. Add the onion powder and stir the crawfish gently.
4. Cook the meal for 5 minutes.

Nutrition value/serving: calories 262, fat 10, fiber 0.1, carbs 1, protein 39.9

Seafood Fajita

Prep time: 10 minutes | **Cooking time:** 10 minutes | **Servings:** 2

Ingredients:

- 1 teaspoon chili flakes
- 1 teaspoon ground coriander
- ½ teaspoon salt
- ½ teaspoon dried cilantro
- 10 oz shrimps, peeled
- 1 yellow bell pepper
- 1 white onion, sliced
- 1 teaspoon lemon juice
- 1 tablespoon olive oil
- 1 teaspoon smoked paprika

Directions

1. In the mixing bowl mix up chili flakes, ground coriander, salt, dried cilantro, and shrimps.
2. Shake the mixture well.
3. After this, preheat the air fryer to 400F.
4. Put the sliced onion in the air fryer and cook it for 3 minutes. Meanwhile, slice the bell pepper.
5. Add it in the air fryer and cook the vegetables for 2 minutes more.
6. Then add shrimps and sprinkle the mixture with smoked paprika, olive oil, and lemon juice.
7. Shake it gently and cook for 5 minutes more.
8. Transfer the cooked fajita in the serving plates.

Nutrition value/serving: calories 273, fat 9.8, fiber 2.4, carbs 12.5, protein 33.7

Cajun Spices Shrimps

Prep time: 10 minutes | **Cooking time:** 6 minutes | **Servings:** 2

Ingredients:

- 8 oz shrimps, peeled
- 1 teaspoon Cajun spices
- 1 teaspoon coconut milk
- 1 egg, beaten
- ½ teaspoon salt
- 1 teaspoon olive oil

Directions

1. Sprinkle the shrimps with Cajun spices and salt.
2. In the mixing bowl mix up coconut milk and egg,
3. Dip every shrimp in the egg mixture.
4. Preheat the air fryer to 400F.
5. Place the shrimps in the air fryer and sprinkle with olive oil.
6. Cook the shrimps for 6 minutes. Shake them well after 3 minutes of cooking.

Nutrition value/serving: calories 192, fat 7, fiber 0.1, carbs 2, protein 28.7

Shrimp Bowl

Prep time: 10 minutes | **Cooking time:** 5 minutes |
Servings: 2

Ingredients:

- 3 oz chevre
- 1 teaspoon olive oil
- ½ teaspoon dried basil
- 8 oz shrimps, peeled
- 1 teaspoon coconut oil, melted
- ½ teaspoon salt
- ½ teaspoon chili flakes
- 4 oz celery stalk, chopped

Directions

1. Sprinkle the shrimps with dried basil and melted coconut oil and put in the air fryer.
2. Cook the seafood at 400F for 5 minutes.
3. Meanwhile, crumble the chevre.
4. Put the chopped celery stalk in the salad bowl.
5. Add crumbled chevre, chili flakes, salt, and olive oil.
6. Mix up the salad well and top it with cooked shrimps.

Nutrition value/serving: calories 381, fat 21.8, fiber 0.9, carbs 3.4, protein 39.9

Parm Salmon

Prep time: 10 minutes | **Cooking time:** 7 minutes |
Servings: 2

Ingredients:

- 10 oz salmon fillet
- 1 teaspoon dried thyme
- 1 teaspoon olive oil
- 2 oz Parmesan, grated
- ¼ teaspoon chili powder

Directions

1. Sprinkle the salmon fillet with dried thyme and chili powder.
2. Then brush it with olive oil.
3. Preheat the air fryer to 385F.
4. Place the salmon in the air fryer basket and cook it for 5 minutes.
5. Then flip the fish on another side and top with Parmesan.
6. Cook the fish for 2 minutes more.

Nutrition value/serving: calories 301, fat 17.3, fiber 0.3, carbs 1.5, protein 36.7

SIDE DISHES

Side Dishes

Spiced Cauliflower Rice

Prep time: 8 minutes | **Cooking time:** 10 minutes | **Servings:** 4

Ingredients:

- 3 tablespoon coconut oil
- 1 teaspoon salt
- 1-pound cauliflower
- 1 teaspoon turmeric
- 1 teaspoon garlic powder
- 1 teaspoon ground ginger
- 1 cup water

Directions

1. Wash the cauliflower and chop it roughly.
2. Then place the chopped cauliflower in the blender and blend it till you get the rice texture of the cauliflower.
3. Transfer the cauliflower rice to the mixing bowl.
4. After this, sprinkle the vegetable mixture with the salt, turmeric, garlic powder, and ground ginger.
5. Mix it up.
6. Preheat the air fryer to 370 F.
7. Put the cauliflower rice mixture there.
8. Add the coconut oil and water.
9. Cook the cauliflower rice for 10 minutes.
10. When the time is over – remove the cauliflower rice from the air fryer and strain the excess liquid.
11. Stir it gently.

Nutritional value/serving: calories 122, fat 10.4, fiber 3.1, carbs 7.2, protein 2.5

Cheese and Vegetables Salad

Prep time: 10 minutes | **Cooking time:** 12 minutes | **Servings:** 8

Ingredients:

- 1-pound lean ground beef
- 1 teaspoon salt
- 1 teaspoon paprika
- 1 teaspoon turmeric
- 1 teaspoon chili pepper
- ½ teaspoon chili flakes
- 1 teaspoon ground black pepper
- 8 oz. Provolone cheese
- 1 tablespoon avocado oil
- 1 tomato
- ¼ cup coconut cream
- 1 cup lettuce

Directions

1. Combine the ground beef with the salt, paprika, turmeric, chili pepper, chili flakes, and ground black pepper.
2. Stir the ground meat mixture with the help of the fork.
3. Sprinkle the ground beef mixture with the avocado oil and place it in the air fryer basket tray.
4. Cook the ground beef at 365 F for 12 minutes. Stir it once during the cooking.
5. Meanwhile, chop the tomato roughly and tear the lettuce.
6. Place the vegetables in the big salad bowl.
7. Cut Provolone cheese into the cubes and add them to the lettuce mixture.
8. When the ground beef is cooked – let it chill till the room temperature.
9. Add the ground beef in the lettuce salad.
10. Sprinkle the dish with the coconut cream and stir it using two wooden spatulas.

Nutritional value/serving: calories 230, fat 13.2, fiber 0.6, carbs 2.2, protein 24.8

Asparagus with Flax Seeds

Prep time: 9 minutes | **Cooking time:** 6 minutes | **Servings:** 6

Ingredients:

- 1-pound asparagus
- 1 teaspoon chili powder
- ½ teaspoon ground black pepper
- 1 tablespoon avocado oil
- 1 tablespoon flax seeds

Directions

1. Combine the avocado oil with the salt, chili powder and ground black pepper.
2. Churn the mixture.
3. Preheat the air fryer to 400 F.
4. Place the asparagus in the air fryer basket tray and sprinkle it with the avocado oil-spice mixture.
5. Cook the asparagus for 6 minutes.
6. When the dish is cooked – let it chill for some minutes.

Nutritional value/serving: calories 26, fat 0.8, fiber 2.2, carbs 3.8, protein 2

Parmesan Gratin

Prep time: 15 minutes | **Cooking time:** 13 minutes | **Servings:** 6

Ingredients:

- 2 zucchini
- 1 tablespoon dried dill
- 1 tablespoon almond flour
- 5 oz. Parmesan cheese, shredded
- 1 teaspoon coconut oil

- 1 teaspoon ground black pepper

Directions

1. Combine the dried dill, almond flour, ground black pepper, and shredded cheese in the big bowl together.
2. Shake it gently to make the homogenous mass.
3. Then wash the zucchini and slice them.
4. Then cut the zucchini to make the squares.
5. Spread the air fryer basket tray with the butter and place the zucchini squares there.
6. Preheat the air fryer to 400 F.
7. Sprinkle the zucchini squares with the dried parsley mixture.
8. Cook the zucchini gratin for 13 minutes.
9. When the zucchini gratin is cooked it will have the light brown color of the surface.

Nutritional value/serving: calories 122, fat 8.3, fiber 1.4, carbs 4.6, protein 9.5

Tender Winter Squash Spaghetti

Prep time: 10 minutes | **Cooking time:** 10 minutes | **Servings:** 8

Ingredients:

- 4 tablespoons coconut cream
- 1 cup water
- 1-pound winter squash
- 1 teaspoon salt
- 1 teaspoon ground black pepper
- 1 teaspoon coconut oil

Directions

1. Peel the winter squash and grate it to get the spaghetti.
2. Preheat the air fryer to 400 F.
3. Put the winter squash spaghetti in the air fryer basket tray.
4. Sprinkle it with the water and salt.
5. Add the ground black pepper and cook the dish for 10 minutes.
6. When the time is over – strain the excess liquid from the winter squash spaghetti.
7. Then add the coconut oil and coconut cream and stir it.

Nutritional value/serving: calories 46, fat 2.4, fiber 1.1, carbs 6.5, protein 0.7

Tender Mash

Prep time: 10 minutes | **Cooking time:** 12 minutes | **Servings:** 7

Ingredients:

- 1-pound Italian dark leaf kale
- 7 oz. Cheddar cheese, shredded
- 1 teaspoon salt
- 1 cup coconut cream
- 1 teaspoon butter
- 1 teaspoon ground black pepper
- 4 oz chive stems, diced

Directions

1. Chop the kale carefully and place it in the air fryer basket tray.
2. Sprinkle the chopped kale with the salt, butter, ground black pepper, diced chives, and coconut cream.
3. Preheat the air fryer to 250 F.
4. Cook the kale for 12 minutes.
5. When the time is over – mix the kale with Cheddar cheese and stir carefully to make it homogenous.

Nutritional value/serving: calories 217, fat 18.4, fiber 2.1, carbs 6.1, protein 9.1

Buttery Celery Stalk

Prep time: 10 minutes | **Cooking time:** 8 minutes | **Servings:** 6

Ingredients:

- 1-pound celery stalk
- 1 tablespoon butter
- 1 cup water
- 2 tablespoons coconut cream
- 1 teaspoon salt
- 1 tablespoon paprika

Directions

1. Chop the celery stalk roughly.
2. Pour the water into the air fryer basket.
3. Preheat the air fryer to 365F.
4. Add the chopped celery stalk, butter, salt, paprika, and coconut cream.
5. Mix the vegetable mixture.
6. Cook the celery for 8 minutes more.
7. When the time is over – the celery stalk should be very soft.

Nutritional value/serving: calories 44, fat 3.4, fiber 1.8, carbs 3.2, protein 0.8

White Mushrooms with Garlic Gravy

Prep time: 10 minutes | **Cooking time:** 12 minutes | **Servings:** 4

Ingredients:

- 9 oz white mushrooms
- 1 teaspoon garlic, sliced
- 3 oz white onion, diced
- 1 cup coconut cream
- 1 teaspoon butter
- 1 teaspoon avocado oil

- 1 teaspoon chili flakes

Directions

1. Slice the white mushrooms.
2. Sprinkle the white mushrooms with the chili flakes.
3. After this, preheat the air fryer to 400 F.
4. Pour the avocado oil in the air fryer basket tray.
5. Then add the sliced mushrooms and cook the vegetables for 5 minutes.
6. After this, add the coconut cream, butter, sliced garlic, and mix the mushroom gently with the help of the spatula.
7. Cook the dish for 7 minutes at 365 F.
8. When the time is over – stir the side dish carefully.

Nutritional value/serving: calories 171, fat 15.6, fiber 2.5, carbs 7.7, protein 3.7

Vegetables and Spices Stew

Prep time: 10 minutes | **Cooking time:** 13 minutes | Servings: 6

Ingredients:

- 1 eggplant
- 1 zucchini
- 1 celery stalk, chopped
- 1 green bell pepper
- 2 garlic cloves, peeled
- 1 teaspoon turmeric
- 1 teaspoon dried dill
- 1 teaspoon dried parsley
- 1 cup water
- ½ cup heavy cream
- 1 teaspoon kosher salt

Directions

1. Cut the zucchini and eggplant into the cubes.
2. Then sprinkle the vegetables with the dried parsley, dried dill, paprika, and turmeric. Add celery stalk.
3. Chop the garlic cloves.
4. Then chop the green pepper.
5. Preheat the air fryer to 390 F.
6. Pour the water into the air fryer and add the eggplants.
7. Cook the eggplants for 2 minutes.
8. After this, add the chopped green pepper.
9. Then add the chopped garlic cloves and heavy cream.
10. Cook the stew for 11 minutes more at the same temperature.

Nutritional value/serving: calories 69, fat 4, fiber 3.5, carbs 6.1, protein 1.7

Green Beans Stew

Prep time: 10 minutes | **Cooking time:** 12 minutes | Servings: 4

Ingredients:

- 1 cup green beans
- 6 oz. Cheddar cheese, shredded
- 7 oz. Provolone cheese, shredded
- ¼ cup coconut cream
- 1 zucchini
- 1 teaspoon salt
- 1 teaspoon paprika
- 1 tablespoon butter

Directions

1. Cut the zucchini into the cubes and sprinkle with the paprika and salt.
2. Then toss the butter in the air fryer basket tray.
3. Add the zucchini cubes in the butter.
4. Preheat the air fryer to 400 F and cook the zucchini for 6 minutes.
5. Then add the green beans, shredded Cheddar cheese, and cayenne pepper.
6. After this, sprinkle the casserole with the shredded Provolone cheese.
7. Pour the coconut cream.
8. Cook the casserole for 6 minutes more at 400 F.
9. When the casserole is cooked – let it chill well.

Nutritional value/serving: calories 391, fat 30.6, fiber 1.7, carbs 6.5, protein 24.5

Lemon Radishes

Prep time: 5 minutes | **Cooking time:** 15 minutes | Servings: 4

Ingredients:

- 2 cups radishes, halved
- 1 tablespoon avocado oil
- 2 tablespoons lemon juice
- 2 tablespoons dill, chopped

Directions

1. In a bowl, mix the radishes with the remaining ingredients except the dill, toss and put them in your air fryer's basket.
2. Cook at 400 degrees F for 15 minutes, divide between plates, sprinkle the dill on top and serve as a side dish.

Nutritional value/serving: calories 20, fat 0.6, fiber 1.3, carbs 3.2, protein 0.8

Tender Leeks

Prep time: 5 minutes | **Cooking time:** 10 minutes | Servings: 4

Ingredients:

- 10 oz leek, chopped
- 2 tablespoons cream cheese
- 1 tablespoon coconut oil, melted
- 1 teaspoon ground coriander
- ¼ teaspoon salt

Directions

1. Sprinkle the leek with salt and ground coriander and transfer in the air fryer.
2. Add coconut oil and gently stir the ingredients.
3. After this, cook the leek for 5 minutes at 375F. Stir the vegetables well and add cream cheese.
4. Cook the meal for 5 minutes more. Serve the cooked leek with cream cheese gravy.

Nutritional value/serving: calories 90, fat 5.4, fiber 1.3, carbs 10.2, protein 1.4

Green Cabbage Bowl

Prep time: 5 minutes | **Cooking time:** 15 minutes | Servings: 4

Ingredients:

- 6 cups green cabbage, shredded
- 6 radishes, sliced
- ½ cup kale, chopped
- 2 tablespoons apple cider vinegar
- 1 teaspoon lemon juice
- 3 tablespoons avocado oil
- ½ teaspoon hot paprika

Directions

1. Put all ingredients in the air fryer basket.
2. Cook the meal at 380F for 15 minutes. Divide between plates and serve as a side dish.

Nutritional value/serving: calories 47, fat 1.5, fiber 3.3, carbs 7.9, protein 1.8

Greek Style Bread Bites

Prep time: 15 minutes | **Cooking time:** 4 minutes | Servings: 6

Ingredients:

- 1 cup Mozzarella, shredded
- 2 tablespoons Greek yogurt
- 1 egg, beaten
- ½ teaspoon baking powder
- ½ cup coconut flour
- 1 teaspoon coconut oil, melted

Directions

1. In the mixing bowl mix up Mozzarella and yogurt.

2. Microwave the mixture for 2 minutes. After this, mix up baking powder, coconut flour, and egg. Combine together the coconut flour mixture and melted Mozzarella mixture.
3. Stir it with the help of the spatula until smooth. Refrigerate the dough for 10 minutes. Then cut it on 6 pieces and roll up to get the flatbread pieces.
4. Air fryer the bread for 3 minutes at 400F. Then brush it with melted coconut oil and cook for 1 minute more or until the bread is light brown.

Nutritional value/serving: calories 72, fat 3.4, fiber 4, carbs 7.2, protein 3.8

Dill Radishes

Prep time: 5 minutes | **Cooking time:** 15 minutes | Servings: 4

Ingredients:

- 20 radishes, halved
- 1 tablespoon dried dill
- 1 tablespoon garlic powder
- 2 tablespoons avocado oil

Directions

1. Put all ingredients in the air fryer basket and mix them well.
2. Cook the meal at 370 degrees F for 15 minutes.

Nutritional value/serving: calories 22, fat 1, fiber 1, carbs 3.1, protein 0.8

Spiced Paneer

Prep time: 10 minutes | **Cooking time:** 6 minutes | Servings: 4

Ingredients:

- 1 cup paneer, cubed
- 2 spring onions, chopped
- ½ teaspoon ground cumin
- 1 tablespoon lemon juice
- ½ teaspoon fresh cilantro, chopped
- 1 tablespoon avocado oil
- ¼ teaspoon low sodium tomato paste
- ½ teaspoon minced garlic
- ½ teaspoon red chili powder
- ¼ teaspoon garam masala powder
- ¼ teaspoon salt

Directions

1. Chop the onion on 4 cubes.
2. Sprinkle the paneer with ground cumin, lemon juice, cilantro, avocado oil, tomato paste, minced garlic, red chili powder, garam masala, and salt.
3. Massage the paneer cubes with the help of the fingertips to coat them well. After this, string the paneer cubes, and onion on the skewers.

4. Preheat the air fryer to 385F. Place the paneer skewers in the air fryer basket and cook them for 3 minutes from each side.

Nutritional value/serving: calories 11, fat 0.6, fiber 0.5, carbs 1.3, protein 0.3

Aromatic Tomatoes

Prep time: 5 minutes | **Cooking time:** 15 minutes | Servings: 4

Ingredients:

- 4 tomatoes, halved
- ½ teaspoon chili powder
- ½ teaspoon garlic powder
- ½ teaspoon dried thyme
- ½ teaspoon oregano, dried
- 1 tablespoon basil, chopped
- ½ cup Cheddar cheese, grated
- Cooking spray

Directions

1. In a bowl, mix all the ingredients except the cooking spray and Cheddar cheese.
2. Arrange the tomatoes in the air fryer basket and sprinkle Cheddar cheese on top and grease with cooking spray.
3. Cook at 370 degrees F for 15 minutes.

Nutritional value/serving: calories 82, fat 5, fiber 1.8, carbs 5.6, protein 4.8

Bacon with Tender Green Beans

Prep time: 15 minutes | **Cooking time:** 13 minutes | Servings: 4

Ingredients:

- 1 cup green beans, trimmed
- 4 oz bacon, sliced
- ¼ teaspoon ground nutmeg
- 1 tablespoon olive oil

Directions

1. Wrap the green beans in the sliced bacon. After this, sprinkle the vegetables with ground nutmeg and olive oil.
2. Preheat the air fryer to 385F.
3. Carefully arrange the green beans in the air fryer in one layer and cook them for 5 minutes.
4. Then flip the green beans on another side and cook for 8 minutes more.

Nutritional value/serving: calories 193, fat 15.4, fiber 1, carbs 2.4, protein 11

Lime Artichokes

Prep time: 5 minutes | **Cooking time:** 15 minutes | Servings: 4

Ingredients:

- 12 ounces artichoke hearts
- Juice of ½ lime
- 4 tablespoons coconut oil, melted
- 2 tablespoons tarragon, chopped

Directions

1. In a bowl, mix all the ingredients, toss, transfer the artichokes to your air fryer's basket and cook at 370 degrees F for 15 minutes.

Nutritional value/serving: calories 160, fat 13.8, fiber 4.7, carbs 9.4, protein 3

Parsley Ravioli

Prep time: 20 minutes | **Cooking time:** 8 minutes | Servings: 6

Ingredients:

- 4 tablespoons almond flour
- 2 tablespoons coconut flour
- 1 tablespoon xanthan gum
- ½ teaspoon baking powder
- 1 egg, beaten
- 1 tablespoon water
- 1 teaspoon lemon juice
- 4 tablespoons cream cheese
- ½ teaspoon garlic powder
- ½ teaspoon dried parsley
- 1 egg yolk, whisked
- Cooking spray

Directions

1. Make the dough: mix up almond flour, coconut flour, xanthan gum, baking powder, egg, water, and lemon juice.
2. Then knead the dough with the help of the fingertips until it is soft and non-sticky.
3. Roll up the dough and cut it on the ravioli squares.
4. Make the ravioli filling: mix up dried ill, ground nutmeg, garlic powder, and cream cheese.
5. Then fill the dough squats with cream cheese.
6. Top the cheese with another ravioli dough squares. Secure the edges. Brush the ravioli with egg yolk. Preheat the air fryer to 375F.
7. Then spray the air fryer basket with cooking spray and place the ravioli inside in one layer.
8. Cook the meal for 4 minutes from each side or until they are light brown.

Nutritional value/serving: calories 104, fat 6.8, fiber 5.5, carbs 7.7, protein 3.6

Cheddar Artichokes

Prep time: 5 minutes | **Cooking time:** 15 minutes | **Servings:** 4

Ingredients:

- 2 tablespoon avocado oil
- 12 ounces artichoke hearts
- 4 spring onions, chopped
- ½ cup Cheddar cheese, grated

Directions

1. In a bowl, mix artichoke hearts with the oil and spring onions and toss.
2. Put the artichokes in your air fryer's basket, sprinkle Cheddar all over and cook at 370 degrees F for 15 minutes.

Nutritional value/serving: calories 111, fat 5.7, fiber 5.3, carbs 10.6, protein 6.7

Provolone Samosa

Prep time: 25 minutes | **Cooking time:** 20 minutes | **Servings:** 6

Ingredients:

- 1 teaspoon garlic, diced
- ¼ teaspoon ground ginger
- 1 teaspoon olive oil
- 1 teaspoon ground turmeric
- ½ teaspoon ground coriander
- ½ teaspoon chili flakes
- 1 cup spinach, chopped
- 3 spring onions, chopped
- 1 teaspoon keto tomato sauce
- 1 cup Provolone cheese, shredded
- ½ cup coconut flour
- ½ teaspoon baking powder
- Cooking spray

Directions

1. Preheat the olive oil in the skillet. Add garlic and ground ginger. Cook the ingredients for 2 minutes over the medium heat. Stir them well.
2. Then add 1 teaspoon of ground turmeric, ground coriander, and chili flakes.
3. Add spinach and stir the mixture well. Add spring onions and tomato sauce. Stir the mixture well and cook it with the closed lid for 10 minutes over the low heat. The spinach mixture should be very soft.
4. Cool the spinach mixture.
5. Meanwhile, make the samosa dough: microwave the cheese until it is melted. Then mix it up with coconut flour and baking powder. Knead the soft dough and put it on the baking paper.
6. Cover the dough with the second baking paper and roll-up. Then cut the flat dough on the triangles.

Place the spinach mixture on every triangle and fold them in the shape of the samosa.

7. Secure the edges of samosa well. Preheat the air fryer to 375F. Spray the air fryer basket with cooking spray. Put the samosa in the air fryer in one layer and cook for 5 minutes.
8. Then flip samosa on another side and cook it for 5 minutes or until the meal is light brown.

Nutritional value/serving: calories 93, fat 2.8, fiber 8.4, carbs 3.3, protein 3

Ginger Endives and Scallions

Prep time: 5 minutes | **Cooking time:** 20 minutes | **Servings:** 4

Ingredients:

- 2 scallions, chopped
- 1 oz ginger, grated
- 1 tablespoon avocado oil
- Salt and black pepper to the taste
- 1 teaspoon chili sauce
- 1 endive, trimmed and roughly shredded

Directions

1. Grease the air fryer basket with the oil, add all the ingredients, toss, introduce in the air fryer and cook at 370 degrees F for 20 minutes.

Nutritional value/serving: calories 33, fat 0.7, fiber 4.3, carbs 6.2, protein 1.8

Broccoli Nuggets

Prep time: 15 minutes | **Cooking time:** 4 minutes | **Servings:** 2

Ingredients:

- 1 egg
- 1 cup broccoli, shredded
- 1 tablespoon coconut flour
- ¼ teaspoon salt
- 1 teaspoon ground turmeric
- 2 oz Parmesan cheese, grated
- Cooking spray

Directions

1. Crack the egg in the bowl and whisk it. Add shredded broccoli, coconut flour, and salt. Mix up the mixture until it is homogenous.
2. Then add Parmesan cheese and turmeric, and stir it until smooth. Make the small balls and press them gently with the help of the fingertips in the shape of nuggets.
3. Preheat the air fryer to 395F. Place the cauli nuggets in the air fryer basket and spray them with cooking spray.
4. Cook the nuggets for 2 minutes from each side.

Cook the nuggets for 2 extra minutes for a saturated golden color.

Nutritional value/serving: calories 172, fat 9.5, fiber 3.9, carbs 5.9, protein 14.2

Coriander Artichokes

Prep time: 5 minutes | **Cooking time:** 15 minutes | Servings: 4

Ingredients:

- 12 ounces artichoke hearts
- ½ teaspoon avocado oil
- 1 teaspoon coriander, ground
- 1 tablespoon apple cider vinegar

Directions

1. Mix all the ingredients and transfer in the air fryer basket.
2. Cook the meal at 370 degrees F for 15 minutes.

Nutritional value/serving: calories 42, fat 0.2, fiber 4.6, carbs 8.3, protein 2.8

Fragrant Tofu

Prep time: 10 minutes | **Cooking time:** 7 minutes | Servings: 3

Ingredients:

- 1 cup tofu, cubed
- 1 tablespoon apple cider vinegar
- 2 tablespoons olive oil
- ¼ teaspoon ground turmeric
- ¼ teaspoon chili flakes

Directions

1. In the mixing bowl mix up apple cider vinegar, olive oil, ground turmeric, and chili flakes.
2. Then coat the tofu in the apple cider vinegar mixture well. Preheat the air fryer to 400F.
3. Put the tofu cubes and all the oily liquid in the air fryer. Cook the tofu for 5 minutes. Then shake it well and cook for 2 minutes more.

Nutritional value/serving: calories 141, fat 12.9, fiber 0.8, carbs 1.6, protein 6.9

Tender Garlic Mushroom

Prep time: 5 minutes | **Cooking time:** 15 minutes | Servings: 4

Ingredients:

- 1 pound brown mushrooms
- 1 teaspoon avocado oil
- 4 garlic cloves, minced
- ½ teaspoon ground paprika

Directions

1. In a bowl, combine all the ingredients and toss.

2. Put the mushrooms in your air fryer's basket and cook at 370 degrees F for 15 minutes.

Nutritional value/serving: calories 37, fat 0.3, fiber 0.9, carbs 5.9, protein 3.1

Onion and Broccoli Patties

Prep time: 15 minutes | **Cooking time:** 10 minutes | Servings: 2

Ingredients:

- ¼ cup broccoli, shredded
- 1 egg yolk
- ½ teaspoon ground turmeric
- ½ white onion, diced
- ¼ teaspoon salt
- 2 oz Cheddar cheese, shredded
- ¼ teaspoon baking powder
- 1 teaspoon coconut cream
- 1 tablespoon coconut flakes
- Cooking spray

Directions

1. Squeeze the shredded broccoli and put it in the bowl.
2. Add egg yolk, ground turmeric, onion, baking powder, salt, coconut cream, and coconut flakes.
3. Then melt Cheddar cheese and add it in the broccoli mixture. Stir the ingredients until you get the smooth mass. After this, make the medium size broccoli patties.
4. Preheat the air fryer to 365F. Spray the air fryer basket with cooking spray and put the patties inside. Cook them for 5 minutes from each side.

Nutritional value/serving: calories 173, fat 13.2, fiber 1.3, carbs 5.2, protein 9.2

Artichokes and Spinach Sauté

Prep time: 5 minutes | **Cooking time:** 15 minutes | Servings: 4

Ingredients:

- 10 ounces artichoke hearts, halved
- 1 teaspoon garlic powder
- 2 cups baby spinach
- ¼ cup water
- 2 teaspoons lime juice

Directions

1. In a pan that fits your air fryer, mix all the ingredients, toss, introduce in the fryer and cook at 370 degrees F for 15 minutes.

Nutritional value/serving: calories 40, fat 0.2, fiber 4.2, carbs 8.7, protein 2.9

Almond Cauliflower Rice

Prep time: 10 minutes | **Cooking time:** 8 minutes |
Servings: 4

Ingredients:

- 2 cup cauliflower, shredded
- ½ teaspoon lemon juice
- ¼ teaspoon salt
- 1 tablespoon ricotta cheese
- ½ teaspoon pumpkin seeds, crushed
- 1 tablespoon organic almond milk
- 1 teaspoon butter, melted

Directions

1. In the bowl mix up butter, cauliflower, lemon juice, salt, and pumpkin seeds. Transfer the mixture in the baking pan for the air fryer.
2. Add almond milk and mix up the vegetable mixture until homogenous. Cover it with the foil. Preheat the air fryer to 375F. Place the pan in the preheated air fryer and cook for 8 minutes.
3. Then remove the pan from the air fryer and add ricotta cheese. Stir the cooked cauliflower rice well.

Nutritional value/serving: calories 25, fat 2.3, fiber 0.1, carbs 0.5, protein 0.6

SNACKS AND
APPETIZERS

Snacks and Appetizers

Anchovies in Almond Flour

Prep time: 20 minutes | **Cooking time:** 6 minutes | **Servings:** 4

Ingredients:

- 1-pound anchovies
- ¼ cup almond flour
- 2 eggs, beaten
- 1 teaspoon salt
- 1 teaspoon ground black pepper
- 1 tablespoon apple cider vinegar
- 1 tablespoon avocado oil

Directions

1. Trim and wash anchovies if needed and put in the big bowl.
2. Add salt and ground black pepper. Mix up the anchovies.
3. Then add eggs and stir the fish until you get a homogenous mixture.
4. After this coat every anchovies fish in the almond flour.
5. Brush the air fryer pan with avocado oil.
6. Place the anchovies in the pan in one layer.
7. Preheat the air fryer to 400F.
8. Put the pan with anchovies in the air fryer and cook them for 6 minutes or until anchovies are golden brown.

Nutrition value/serving: calories 286, fat 14.5, fiber 0.5, carbs 1.1, protein 36

Cod Tacos Bowl

Prep time: 15 minutes | **Cooking time:** 10 minutes | **Servings:** 4

Ingredients:

- 7 oz cod fillet
- 1 teaspoon arrowroot powder
- 1 teaspoon ground paprika
- ½ teaspoon salt
- ¼ teaspoon ground cumin
- ½ teaspoon minced garlic
- 1 teaspoon lime juice
- 4 oz purple cabbage, shredded
- 1 jalapeno, sliced
- 1 tablespoon coconut cream
- Cooking spray

Directions

1. Sprinkle the cod fillet with arrowroot powder, ground paprika, ground cumin, minced garlic, and salt.
2. Preheat the air fryer to 385F.
3. Spray the cod fillet with cooking spray and place it in the air fryer.
4. Cook the fish for 10 minutes.
5. Meanwhile, in the bowl mix up shredded cabbage, jalapeno pepper, and lime juice.
6. When the cod fillet is cooked, chop it roughly.
7. Put the shredded cabbage mixture in the serving bowls.
8. Top them with chopped cod.
9. Sprinkle the meal with a coconut cream.

Nutrition value/serving: calories 64, fat 1.5, fiber 1.1, carbs 3.5, protein 9.5

Mahi Mahi Patties

Prep time: 15 minutes | **Cooking time:** 11 minutes | **Servings:** 4

Ingredients:

- ½ cup cauliflower, shredded
- 1 tablespoon flax meal
- 1 egg, beaten
- 1 teaspoon ground cumin
- 1 oz Parmesan, shredded
- ½ teaspoon salt
- 6 oz Mahi Mahi, chopped
- Cooking spray

Directions

1. In the mixing bowl mix up flax meal, egg, ground cumin, salt, cauliflower, and chopped Mahi Mahi.
2. Stir the ingredients gently with the help of the fork and add shredded Parmesan cheese. Stir the mixture until homogenous.
3. Then make 4 patties.
4. Preheat the air fryer to 390F.
5. Place the Mahi Mahi cakes in the air fryer and spray them gently with cooking spray.
6. Cook the fish cakes for 5 minutes and then flip on another side.
7. Cook the fish cakes for 6 minutes more.

Nutrition value/serving: calories 98, fat 3.8, fiber 0.9, carbs 1.7, protein 14.5

Tender Squid Tubes

Prep time: 20 minutes | **Cooking time:** 6 minutes | **Servings:** 4

Ingredients:

- 4 squid tubes, trimmed
- 1 teaspoon ground paprika
- ½ teaspoon ground turmeric
- ½ teaspoon garlic powder
- ½ cup broccoli shredded
- 1 egg, beaten

- ½ teaspoon salt
- Cooking spray

Directions

1. Clean the squid tubes if needed.
2. After this, in the mixing bowl mix up ground paprika, turmeric, garlic powder, shredded broccoli, and salt.
3. Stir the mixture gently and add a beaten egg. Mix the mixture up.
4. Then fill the squid tubes with shredded broccoli mixture.
5. Secure the edges of the squid tubes with toothpicks.
6. Preheat the air fryer to 390F.
7. Place the stuffed squid tubes in the air fryer and spray with cooking spray.
8. Cook the meal for 6 minutes.

Nutrition value/serving: calories 83, fat 2.7, fiber 0.6, carbs 1.6, protein 13.8

Bacon Cheese Balls

Prep time: 10 minutes | **Cooking time:** 10 minutes | Servings: 6

Ingredients:

- 5 oz bacon, sliced
- 10 oz mozzarella
- ¼ teaspoon dried oregano
- ¼ teaspoon ground turmeric

Directions

1. Sprinkle the sliced bacon with the ground turmeric and oregano.
2. Then wrap the mozzarella balls in the sliced bacon.
3. Secure the mozzarella balls with the toothpicks.
4. Preheat the air fryer to 360 F.
5. Put the mozzarella balls in the air fryer rack and cook for 10 minutes.

Nutritional value/serving: calories 262, fat 18.2, fiber 0.1, carbs 2.1, protein 22.1

Aromatic Cilantro Calamari Rings

Prep time: 10 minutes | **Cooking time:** 4 minutes | Servings: 4

Ingredients:

- 1 teaspoon ground turmeric
- ¼ teaspoon salt
- 10 oz calamari
- ½ teaspoon dried cilantro
- ½ teaspoon dried dill
- 1 teaspoon lemon juice
- 1 teaspoon coconut oil, melted
- ¼ teaspoon ground coriander
- 1 teaspoon olive oil

Directions

1. Trimmed and wash the calamari.
2. Then slice it into rings and sprinkle with ground turmeric, salt, dried cilantro, ground coriander, and lemon juice.
3. Add olive oil and stir the calamari rings.
4. Preheat the air fryer to 400F.
5. Put the calamari rings in the air fryer basket and cook them for 2 minutes.
6. When the time is finished, shake them well and cook for 2 minutes more.
7. Transfer the calamari rings in the big bowl and sprinkle with coconut oil.

Nutrition value/serving: calories 35, fat 2.9, fiber 0.2, carbs 1, protein 1.4

Crab Balls

Prep time: 15 minutes | **Cooking time:** 6 minutes | Servings: 6

Ingredients:

- 1 teaspoon Creole seasonings
- 4 tablespoons coconut flour
- ¼ teaspoon baking powder
- 1 teaspoon lemon juice
- ¼ teaspoon onion powder
- 1 teaspoon dried parsley
- 1 teaspoon ghee
- 13 oz crab meat, finely chopped
- 1 egg, beaten

Directions

1. In the mixing bowl mix up crab meat, egg, dried parsley, ghee, onion powder, lemon juice, baking powder, and Creole seasonings.
2. Then add coconut flour and stir the mixture with the help of the fork until it is homogenous.
3. Make the small balls.
4. Preheat the air fryer to 390F.
5. Put the balls in the air fryer basket and spray with cooking spray.
6. Cook them for 3 minutes.
7. Then flip them on another side and cook for 3 minutes more or until the balls are golden brown.

Nutrition value/serving: calories 92, fat 3.2, fiber 1.7, carbs 4, protein 9.3

Wrapped Lobster Tails

Prep time: 10 minutes | **Cooking time:** 6 minutes | Servings: 4

Ingredients:

- 4 kale leaves
- ½ teaspoon taco seasonings

- 4 lobster tails
- ½ teaspoon ground coriander
- ½ teaspoon chili flakes
- 1 tablespoon cream cheese
- 1 teaspoon olive oil

Directions

1. Peel the lobster tails and sprinkle with ground coriander, taco seasonings, and chili flakes.
2. Arrange the lobster tails in the air fryer basket and sprinkle with olive oil.
3. Cook them for 6 minutes at 380F.
4. After this, remove the cooked lobster tails from the air fryer and chop them roughly. Transfer the lobster tails into the bowl.
5. Add cream cheese and mix.
6. Place the lobster mixture on the kale leaves and fold them.

Nutrition value/serving: calories 137, fat 2.7, fiber 1.3, carbs 9, protein 18.9

Broccoli Crispy Florets

Prep time: 15 minutes | **Cooking time:** 16 minutes | Servings: 8

Ingredients:

- 18 oz broccoli
- 1 cup coconut cream
- 1 teaspoon salt
- ½ teaspoon ground black pepper
- 1 teaspoon turmeric
- 1 egg
- 2 tablespoons coconut flour
- 1 teaspoon oregano
- ½ tablespoon olive oil

Directions

1. Wash the broccoli carefully and separate it into the medium florets.
2. After this beat the egg in the big bowl and whisk it.
3. Add the salt, ground black pepper, turmeric, coconut flour, coconut milk, and oregano.
4. Whisk the mixture till you get the smooth batter.
5. Then coat the broccoli florets with the coconut cream batter.
6. Preheat the air fryer to 360 F.
7. Place the coated broccoli florets in the air fryer basket tray.
8. Cook the vegetables for 12 minutes.
9. After this, increase the temperature to 390 F and cook the snack for 4 minutes more.

Nutritional value/serving: calories 123, fat 9.3, fiber 3.7, carbs 8.3, protein 3.7

Cod Fries

Prep time: 10 minutes | **Cooking time:** 6 minutes | Servings: 4

Ingredients:

- 10 oz cod fillet
- 1 tablespoon almond flour
- 1 tablespoon coconut flakes
- 1 egg, beaten
- 1 teaspoon ground paprika
- ½ teaspoon salt
- 1 tablespoon coconut cream
- 1 teaspoon olive oil

Directions

1. Cut the cod fillets on the fries strips.
2. After this, in the mixing bowl mix up almond flour, coconut flakes, ground paprika, and salt.
3. In the other bowl mix up egg and coconut cream.
4. After this, dip the fish fries in the egg mixture. Then coat them in the almond flour mixture.
5. Repeat the steps again.
6. Preheat the air fryer to 400F.
7. Put the fish fries in the air fryer basket in one layer and sprinkle them with olive oil.
8. Cook the meal for 3 minutes.
9. Then flip the fish fries on another side and cook for 3 minutes more.

Nutrition value/serving: calories 137, fat 7.8, fiber 1.1, carbs 2.3, protein 15.8

Keto Gumbo

Prep time: 10 minutes | **Cooking time:** 12 minutes | Servings: 4

Ingredients:

- 10 oz shrimps, peeled
- 1 teaspoon avocado oil
- 1 teaspoon ground black pepper
- 1 white onion, diced
- 1 jalapeno pepper, chopped
- ½ cup water
- 1 teaspoon chili flakes
- ½ teaspoon dried cilantro
- ½ teaspoon salt

Directions

1. Preheat the air fryer to 400F.
2. Meanwhile, in the mixing bowl mix up onion, jalapeno pepper, avocado oil, ground black pepper, and salt.
3. Put the ingredients in the air fryer.
4. Cook it for 2 minutes.
5. After this, add dried cilantro, and shrimps.
6. Add water.

7. Stir the ingredients gently and cook the meal for 6 minutes at 400F.

Nutrition value/serving: calories 99, fat 1.4, fiber 0.9, carbs 4.3, protein 16.6

Coconut Cod with Smoked Paprika

Prep time: 10 minutes | **Cooking time:** 12 minutes | Servings: 2

Ingredients:

• 8 oz cod fillet
• 1 teaspoon heavy cream
• 1 teaspoon almond flour
• ½ teaspoon salt
• ¼ teaspoon smoked paprika
• ½ teaspoon dried basil
• ½ teaspoon coconut oil, melted
• ¼ teaspoon ground cumin

Directions

1. Rub the cod fillet with ground cumin, dried basil, smoked paprika, and salt.
2. Then dip it in the heavy cream.
3. Cut the cod fillet on 2 servings.
4. After this, sprinkle every cod fillet with almond flour gently.
5. Preheat the air fryer to 385F.
6. Sprinkle the air fryer basket with coconut oil and put the cod fillets inside.
7. Cook the fillets for 6 minutes from every side.

Nutrition value/serving: calories 118, fat 3.7, fiber 0.3, carbs 0.6, protein 20.7

Fish en Papillote

Prep time: 15 minutes | **Cooking time:** 15 minutes | Servings: 4

Ingredients:

• 12 oz salmon fillet
• 1 zucchini, peeled
• ½ white onion, sliced
• 1 tablespoon ghee, melted
• 1 teaspoon peppercorns
• ½ teaspoon salt
• ½ teaspoon ground black pepper
• 1 teaspoon tarragon

Directions

1. Cut the salmon fillet on 4 servings.
2. Then make the parchment pockets and place the fish fillets in the parchment pockets.
3. Sprinkle the salmon with salt, ground black pepper, tarragon.
4. After this, top the fish with sliced onion, peppercorns, and ghee.

5. Slice the zucchini and place it over the ghee.
6. Preheat the air fryer to 385F.
7. Arrange the salmon pockets in the air fryer in one layer and cook them for 15 minutes.

Nutrition value/serving: calories 156, fat 8.6, fiber 1, carbs 3.3, protein 17.3

Garlic Haddock with Celery Root

Prep time: 10 minutes | **Cooking time:** 16 minutes | Servings: 2

Ingredients:

• 7 oz haddock fillet
• 2 tablespoons coconut oil, melted
• 1 teaspoon minced garlic
• ½ teaspoon salt
• 1 teaspoon fresh dill, chopped
• ½ teaspoon ground celery root

Directions

1. Cut the fish fillet on 2 servings.
2. In the shallow bowl mix up coconut oil and minced garlic.
3. Then add salt, celery root, and fresh dill.
4. After this, carefully brush the fish fillets with the coconut oil mixture.
5. Then wrap every fillet in the foil.
6. Preheat the air fryer to 385F.
7. Put the wrapped haddock fillets in the air fryer and cook for 16 minutes.

Nutrition value/serving: calories 232, fat 14.6, fiber 0.1, carbs 0.8, protein 24.2

Eggplants Bites

Prep time: 15 minutes | **Cooking time:** 8 minutes | Servings: 9

Ingredients:

• 2 eggplants
• 1 tablespoon avocado oil
• 1 teaspoon minced garlic
• ½ teaspoon salt
• 1 teaspoon dried oregano
• 1 teaspoon dried rosemary

Directions

1. Wash the eggplants carefully and slice into the thick circles.
2. After this, combine the avocado oil, minced garlic, salt, dried oregano, and dried rosemary in the bowl.
3. Churn the mixture.
4. After this, brush every eggplants circle with the oil mixture.
5. Preheat the air fryer to 400 F.
6. Place the prepared eggplants circles in the air fryer

rack and cook them for 5 minutes.

7. After this, turn the eggplant circles to another side and cook them for 3 minutes more.
8. When the eggplants are soft and little bit golden brown – they are cooked.

Nutritional value/serving: calories 34, fat 0.5, fiber 4.5, carbs 7.5, protein 1.3

Onion Rings

Prep time: 15 minutes | **Cooking time:** 8 minutes | **Servings:** 10

Ingredients:

- 2 white onions
- ½ teaspoon salt
- ½ cup almond flour
- ½ teaspoon paprika
- ½ teaspoon ground white pepper
- 1 egg
- 1/3 cup coconut cream
- 1 tablespoon olive oil

Directions

1. Peel the white onions and slice them roughly.
2. Then separate the sliced onions into the circles.
3. Beat the egg and whisk it.
4. Sprinkle the whisked egg with the paprika, salt, ground white pepper, and coconut cream.
5. Whisk it well until homogenous.
6. Preheat the air fryer to 360 F.
7. Coat the onion rings in the almond flour.
8. After this, dip the onion circles in the whisked egg mixture.
9. Then coat the onion circles in the almond flour.
10. Spray the air fryer basket tray with the olive oil and place the onion circles there.
11. Cook the onion circles for 8 minutes.
12. When the snack is cooked – let it chill well.

Nutritional value/serving: calories 78, fat 6.6, fiber 1.3, carbs 3.9, protein 2.2

Paprika Zucchini Cakes

Prep time: 10 minutes | **Cooking time:** 10 minutes | **Servings:** 7

Ingredients:

- 1 zucchini, grated
- 1 egg
- 4 tablespoons almond flour
- ½ teaspoon salt
- ½ tablespoon paprika
- 1 teaspoon coconut oil
- 1 oz chive stems
- ½ teaspoon chili flakes

Directions

1. Put the grated zucchini in the big mixing bowl.
2. Beat the egg in the zucchini.
3. Then add almond flour, salt, paprika, diced chives, and chili flakes.
4. Mix the mixture carefully.
5. Preheat the air fryer to 365 F.
6. Put the coconut in the air fryer basket tray and melt it.
7. After this, make the small fritters with the help of the spoon and place them in the melted butter.
8. Cook the fritters for 5 minutes from each side.
9. When the fritters are cooked – chill them well.

Nutritional value/serving: calories 43, fat 3.4, fiber 0.9, carbs 2.1, protein 2.1

Curry Chicken Bites

Prep time: 15 minutes | **Cooking time:** 15 minutes | **Servings:** 8

Ingredients:

- 1-pound chicken fillet
- ½ teaspoon curry powder
- ½ cup coconut cream
- 2 tablespoons coconut flour
- 1 teaspoon olive oil

Directions

1. Chop the chicken fillet into 8 cubes.
2. Place the chicken cubes in the big bowl.
3. Then sprinkle the chicken with curry powder.
4. Mix the chicken up with the help of the hands.
5. After this, combine the coconut cream and coconut flour in the separate bowl.
6. Whisk it well.
7. Preheat the air fryer to 365 F.
8. Place the chicken cubes in the air fryer rack and sprinkle them with the olive oil.
9. Cook the chicken for 15 minutes.
10. When the chicken bites are cooked – chill them well.

Nutritional value/serving: calories 155, fat 8.6, fiber 1.1, carbs 2.2, protein 17

Beef and Tomato Meatballs

Prep time: 10 minutes | **Cooking time:** 13 minutes | **Servings:** 7

Ingredients:

- 1 egg
- 1-pound ground beef
- 1 tablespoon keto tomato puree
- 1 teaspoon salt
- 1 teaspoon ground ginger
- ½ teaspoon ground cumin

- 1 tablespoon coconut oil
- ¼ teaspoon chili flakes

Directions

1. Beat the egg in the bowl.
2. Add the salt, ground ginger, ground cumin, and chili flakes.
3. Mix the mixture up till it is homogenous.
4. After this, add the ground beef and stir it carefully until homogenous.
5. Then preheat the air fryer to 3660 F.
6. Make 7 small meatballs from the ground beef mixture.
7. Then place the meatballs in the air fryer basket tray.
8. Add coconut oil and tomato puree.
9. Cook the meatballs for 13 minutes.
10. Stir the meatballs after 7 minutes of cooking.

Nutritional value/serving: calories 148, fat 6.7, fiber 0.1, carbs 0.3, protein 20.5

Sweet Chicken Wings

Prep time: 15 minutes | **Cooking time:** 12 minutes | Servings: 5

Ingredients:

- 1 teaspoon Erythritol
- 1 teaspoon salt
- 1-pound chicken wings
- 1 teaspoon curry powder
- 1 teaspoon dried oregano
- 1 tablespoon avocado oil

Directions

1. Combine the salt, curry powder, and dried oregano in the bowl and stir it.
2. After this, sprinkle the chicken wings with the spice mixture.
3. Then sprinkle the chicken wings with the Erythritol.
4. Preheat the air fryer to 400 F.
5. Place the prepared chicken wings in the air fryer rack and spray them with the avocado oil.
6. After this, cook the chicken for 12 minutes.
7. When the chicken wings are cooked – place them on the paper towel.

Nutritional value/serving: calories 178, fat 7.2, fiber 0.4, carbs 0.6, protein 26.4

Squash Fries

Prep time: 10 minutes | **Cooking time:** 15 minutes | Servings: 6

Ingredients:

- 2 sweet dumpling squashes
- 1 teaspoon paprika
- ¼ teaspoon ground turmeric

- ¼ teaspoon salt
- 1 tablespoon sesame oil

Directions

1. Peel the sweet dumpling squash and cut it into the strips.
2. Cover the air fryer basket tray with the parchment and place the sweet dumpling squash strips there.
3. Then sprinkle the sweet dumpling squash strips with the ground turmeric, paprika, and salt.
4. Spray the sweet dumpling squash strips with the sesame oil.
5. Preheat the air fryer to 365 F.
6. Cook the sweet dumpling squash fries for 15 minutes. The time can be less or more – depends on the size of the sweet dumpling squash strips.

Nutritional value/serving: calories 31, fat 2.3, fiber 0.5, carbs 2.6, protein 0.4

Zucchini Bites with Parmesan

Prep time: 8 minutes | **Cooking time:** 14 minutes | Servings: 4

Ingredients:

- 1 zucchini
- ½ teaspoon ground paprika
- ¼ teaspoon salt
- 4 oz. Parmesan, sliced
- 1 teaspoon sesame oil

Directions

1. Cut the zucchini into four bites.
2. Then sprinkle the zucchini bites with the paprika, salt, and stir them well.
3. After this, preheat the air fryer to 400 F.
4. Place the eggplants bites in the air fryer basket tray and spray them with the sesame oil.
5. After this, cook the zucchini bites for 13 minutes.
6. Then cover the zucchini bites with the sliced Parmesan.
7. Cook the dish for 1 minute more.
8. Then transfer the zucchini bites on the serving plate and chill them till the cheese started to be solid.

Nutritional value/serving: calories 110, fat 7.3, fiber 0.6, carbs 2.8, protein 9.7

Cumin Zucchini Chips

Prep time: 8 minutes | **Cooking time:** 13 minutes | Servings: 5

Ingredients:

- 2 zucchini
- 1 teaspoon avocado oil
- ½ teaspoon salt
- 1 teaspoon ground cumin

Directions

1. Wash the zucchini carefully and slice it into the chips pieces.
2. Preheat the air fryer to 370 F.
3. Sprinkle the zucchini slices with the salt and cumin.
4. After this, place the zucchini slices in the air fryer rack.
5. Sprinkle the zucchini slices with the oil gently.
6. Cook the zucchini strips for 13 minutes.
7. Turn the zucchini strips into another side during the cooking if desired.
8. When the zucchini chips are cooked let them chill well.
9. Serve the zucchini chips or keep them in the paper bag.

Nutritional value/serving: calories 15, fat 0.4, fiber 0.9, carbs 2.9, protein 1

Rosemary Radish Chips

Prep time: 8 minutes | **Cooking time:** 15 minutes | **Servings:** 12

Ingredients:

• 1-pound radish
• 2 tablespoons avocado oil
• 1 teaspoon salt
• 1 teaspoon dried rosemary

Directions

1. Wash the radish carefully and slice it into the chips size.
2. After this, sprinkle the radish chips with the salt and rosemary.
3. Spray the radish chips with the avocado oil.
4. Preheat the air fryer to 375 F.
5. Place the radish slices in the air fryer rack and cook the chips for 15 minutes.
6. When the radish chips get the desired texture – they are cooked.

Nutritional value/serving: calories 9, fat 0.4, fiber 0.7, carbs 1.5, protein 0.3

Spiced Avocado Fries

Prep time: 10 minutes | **Cooking time:** 10 minutes | **Servings:** 4

Ingredients:

• 1 avocado, pitted
• ½ teaspoon salt
• 1 teaspoon curry powder
• ½ teaspoon paprika
• 1 egg
• 1 tablespoon almond flour
• 1 teaspoon olive oil

Directions

1. Peel the avocado and cut it into the thick strips.
2. Then beat the egg in the bowl and whisk it.
3. Combine the salt, curry powder, paprika, and almond flour.
4. Sprinkle the avocado thick strips with the whisked egg.
5. Then coat every avocado strip into the spice dry mixture.
6. Place the avocado strips in the air fryer rack and spray them with the olive oil.
7. Then set the air fryer to 390 F and cook the avocado fries for 10 minutes.
8. After this, shake the avocado fries gently and cook them for 5 minutes more.

Nutritional value/serving: calories 141, fat 13, fiber 3.8, carbs 5.2, protein 2.8

Mustard Chicken Wings

Prep time: 15 minutes | **Cooking time:** 14 minutes | **Servings:** 4

Ingredients:

• 1-pound chicken wings
• ½ teaspoon salt
• 1 teaspoon minced garlic
• ¼ teaspoon cayenne pepper
• ½ teaspoon ground ginger
• 1 tablespoon mustard
• 1 tablespoon olive oil

Directions

1. Place the chicken wings in the mixing bowl.
2. Sprinkle the chicken wings with the salt, minced garlic, cayenne pepper, ground ginger, oil, and mustard.
3. Mix the chicken wings carefully.
4. Let the chicken wings for 10 minutes to marinate.
5. Preheat the air fryer to 370 F.
6. Place the chicken wings in the air fryer basket tray and cook the dish for 14 minutes.

Nutritional value/serving: calories 261, fat 12.7, fiber 0.5, carbs 1.4, protein 33.6

Oregano Shrimp Tails

Prep time: 10 minutes | **Cooking time:** 14 minutes | **Servings:** 6

Ingredients:

• 1-pound shrimp tails
• 1 tablespoon olive oil
• 1 teaspoon dried oregano
• 2 tablespoons almond flour
• ½ cup heavy cream

- 1 teaspoon chili flakes

Directions

1. Peel the shrimp tails and sprinkle them with the dried oregano.
2. Mix the shrimp tails carefully in the mixing bowl.
3. After this, combine the almond flour, heavy cream, and chili flakes in the separate bowl and whisk it until you get the smooth batter.
4. Then preheat the air fryer to 330 F.
5. Transfer the shrimp tails in the heavy crema batter and stir the seafood carefully.
6. Then spray the air fryer rack and put the shrimp tails there.
7. Cook the shrimp tails for 7 minutes.
8. After this, turn the shrimp tails into another side.
9. Cook the shrimp tails for 7 minutes more.

Nutritional value/serving: calories 198, fat 12, fiber 1.1, carbs 3.6, protein 19.5

Coated Rings

Prep time: 12 minutes | **Cooking time:** 8 minutes | Servings: 4

Ingredients:

- 1 cup coconut flour
- 9 oz calamari, peeled
- 1 egg
- ½ teaspoon lemon zest
- 1 teaspoon apple cider vinegar
- ½ teaspoon turmeric
- ¼ teaspoon salt
- ¼ teaspoon ground black pepper

Directions

1. Wash the calamari.
2. Then slice the calamari into thick rings.
3. Beat the egg in the bowl and whisk it.
4. Sprinkle the whisked egg with the lemon zest, turmeric, salt, and ground black pepper.
5. Sprinkle the calamari rings with the apple cider vinegar.
6. After this, place the calamari rings in the whisked egg and stir it carefully.
7. Leave the calamari rings in the egg mixture for 4 minutes.
8. Then coat the calamari rings in the coconut flour mixture well.
9. Preheat the air fryer to 360 F.
10. Transfer the calamari rings in the air fryer rack.
11. Cook the calamari rings for 8 minutes.

Nutritional value/serving: calories 180, fat 13.4, fiber 3.1, carbs 6.8, protein 8.7

Beef Bombs

Prep time: 15 minutes | **Cooking time:** 14 minutes | Servings: 7

Ingredients:

- 6 oz ground chicken
- 12 oz ground beef
- ½ teaspoon onion powder
- 3 garlic cloves, minced
- 1 tablespoon dried dill
- ½ teaspoon salt
- ½ teaspoon chili powder
- 1 egg
- 1 tablespoon butter

Directions

1. Put the ground chicken and ground beef in the mixing bowl.
2. Add the onion powder, minced garlic, dried dill, salt, and chili powder.
3. Crack the egg into the bowl with the ground meat.
4. Then stir the meat mixture with the help of the hands.
5. Melt butter and add it to the ground meat mixture.
6. Stir it.
7. Leave the ground meat mixture for 5 minutes to rest.
8. Preheat the air fryer to 370 F.
9. Make the small meat bombs from the meat mixture and put them in the air fryer.
10. Cook the meatballs for 14 minutes.

Nutritional value/serving: calories 164, fat 7.2, fiber 0.2, carbs 1, protein 22.8

Nuts Mix

Prep time: 5 minutes | **Cooking time:** 9 minutes | Servings: 4

Ingredients:

- ¼ cup nuts
- ¼ cup walnuts
- ½ cup pecans
- ½ cup almonds
- 1 tablespoon sesame oil
- 1 teaspoon salt

Directions

1. Preheat the air fryer to 320 F.
2. Place the nuts, walnuts, pecans, and almonds in the air fryer.
3. Cook the nut mixture for 8 minutes.
4. Stir the nut mixture s after 4 minutes of the cooking.
5. At the end of the cooking, sprinkle the nut mixture with the sesame oil and salt and shake them well.
6. Cook the nut mixture for 1 minute more.

Nutritional value/serving: calories 210, fat 19.6, fiber 3, carbs 5.7, protein 6.1

VEGETARIAN MEALS

Vegetarian Meals

Spiced Hash Browns

Prep time: 10 minutes | **Cooking time:** 5 minutes |
Servings: 3

Ingredients:

- 2 cups radish, trimmed
- ½ white onion, diced
- ½ teaspoon salt
- ½ teaspoon thyme
- ½ teaspoon ground white pepper
- ½ teaspoon ground paprika
- 1 teaspoon ghee

Directions

1. Chop the radish roughly and mix it up with onion, salt, thyme, ground white pepper, ad paprika.
2. After this, preheat the air fryer to 375F.
3. Put the roughly chopped radish in the air fryer and cook it for 2 minutes.
4. Then add ghee, shake well and cook the vegetables for 3 minutes more.

Nutrition value/serving: calories 359, fat 1.6, fiber 1.9, carbs 4.9, protein 0.8

Zucchini and Flax Meal Patties

Prep time: 15 minutes | **Cooking time:** 10 minutes |
Servings: 4

Ingredients:

- 2 zucchinis, trimmed, grated
- 1 egg, beaten
- ½ teaspoon salt
- 1 teaspoon ground cumin
- ½ teaspoon ground paprika
- 1 teaspoon ricotta cheese
- 3 tablespoons flax meal
- 1 teaspoon sesame oil

Directions

1. Squeeze the juice from the zucchinis and put them in the big bowl.
2. Add egg, salt, ground cumin, ground paprika, flax meal, and ricotta cheese.
3. Stir the mixture well with the help of the spoon.
4. Then make medium size patties from the zucchini mixture.
5. Preheat the air fryer to 385F.
6. Brush the air fryer basket with sesame oil and put the patties inside.
7. Cook them for 5 minutes from each side.

Nutrition value/serving: calories 68, fat 4.5 fiber 2.7, carbs 5.3, protein 4

Green Patties

Prep time: 20 minutes | **Cooking time:** 6 minutes |
Servings: 4

Ingredients:

- 1 ½ cup fresh spinach, chopped
- 3 oz Cheddar cheese, shredded
- 1 egg, beaten
- ¼ cup coconut flour
- ½ teaspoon salt
- Cooking spray

Directions

1. Put the chopped spinach in the blender and blend it until you get a smooth mixture.
2. After this, transfer the grinded spinach in the big bowl.
3. Add shredded cheese, beaten egg, coconut flour, and salt.
4. Stir the spinach mixture with the help of the spoon until it is homogenous.
5. Then make the patties from the spinach mixture.
6. Preheat the air fryer to 400F.
7. Spray the air fryer basket with cooking spray from inside and put the spinach patties.
8. Cook them for 3 minutes and then flip on another side.
9. Cook the patties for 3 minutes more or until they are light brown.

Nutrition value/serving: calories 134, fat 8.9, fiber 3.3, carbs 5.8, protein 8

Tender Cheesy Snap Peas

Prep time: 10 minutes | **Cooking time:** 6 minutes |
Servings: 4

Ingredients:

- 1 cup snap peas, frozen
- 2 oz Provolone cheese, shredded
- 1 teaspoon coconut oil
- ½ teaspoon chili flakes
- ¼ cup water

Directions

1. Sprinkle the snap peas with chili flakes and put in the air fryer baking pan.
2. Add water and coconut oil.
3. Then top the vegetables with shredded Provolone.
4. Preheat the air fryer to 400F.
5. Put the pan with snap peas in the air fryer and cook the meal for 6 minutes.

Nutrition value/serving: calories 89, fat 5.1, fiber 1.9, carbs 5.6, protein 5.6

Tender Fennel Bulb

Prep time: 10 minutes | **Cooking time:** 15 minutes | **Servings:** 2

Ingredients:

• 8 oz fennel bulb
• 1 teaspoon olive oil
• ½ teaspoon salt
• 1 teaspoon smoked paprika

Directions

1. Trim the fennel bulb and cut it into halves.
2. Then sprinkle the fennel bulb with salt, smoked paprika, and olive oil.
3. Preheat the air fryer to 370F.
4. Put the fennel bulb halves in the air fryer and cook them for 15 minutes.

Nutrition value/serving: calories 58, fat 2.7, fiber 3.9, carbs 8.9, protein 1.6

Clove Okra

Prep time: 10 minutes | **Cooking time:** 10 minutes | **Servings:** 4

Ingredients:

• 1-pound okra, trimmed
• 3 oz pancetta, sliced
• ½ teaspoon ground clove
• ½ teaspoon salt
• 1 teaspoon olive oil

Directions

1. Sprinkle okra with ground clove and salt.
2. Then put the vegetables in the air fryer and sprinkle with oil.
3. Chop pancetta roughly.
4. Top the okra with pancetta and cook the meal for 10 minutes at 360F.

Nutrition value/serving: calories 171, fat 10.3, fiber 3.7, carbs 8.9, protein 10.1

Pepper and Cheese Salad

Prep time: 15 minutes | **Cooking time:** 10 minutes | **Servings:** 4

Ingredients:

• 5 oz Mozzarella cheese, crumbled
• 8 oz bell pepper, trimmed
• 1 teaspoon sesame oil
• 1 garlic clove, minced
• ½ teaspoon fresh dill, chopped
• 1 teaspoon apple cider vinegar
• ½ teaspoon lime zest, grated

Directions

1. Clean the seeds from the peppers and cut them into halves.
2. Then sprinkle the peppers with sesame oil and put in the air fryer.
3. Cook them for 10 minutes at 385F. Flip the peppers on another side after 5 minutes of cooking.
4. Meanwhile, mix up minced garlic, fresh dill, apple cider vinegar, and lime zest.
5. Put the cooked peppers on the plate and sprinkle with vinegar mixture.
6. Then top the vegetables with crumbled Mozzarella.

Nutrition value/serving: calories 188, fat 8, fiber 3.3, carbs 9.6, protein 12.5

Squash Bowl

Prep time: 15 minutes | **Cooking time:** 12 minutes | **Servings:** 4

Ingredients:

• 10 oz Kabocha squash
• ½ eggplant, chopped
• ½ white onion, chopped
• 1 teaspoon dried oregano
• 2 teaspoons ghee
• 1 teaspoon salt
• 1 teaspoon ground turmeric

Directions

1. Chop the squash into small cubes and sprinkle with salt and ground turmeric.
2. Put the squash in the bowl, add eggplant, onion, dried oregano, and ghee.
3. Shake the vegetables gently.
4. Preheat the air fryer to 400F.
5. Put the vegetable mixture in the air fryer and cook for 12 minutes. Shake the vegetables after 6 minutes of cooking to avoid burning.

Nutrition value/serving: calories 67, fat 2.3, fiber 3.4, carbs 6.8, protein 1.6

Kohlrabi and Cheese Bowl

Prep time: 10 minutes | **Cooking time:** 20 minutes | **Servings:** 6

Ingredients:

• 12 oz kohlrabi, chopped
• 2 tablespoons heavy cream
• 1 teaspoon salt
• ½ cup Cheddar cheese, shredded
• ¼ cup water
• ½ teaspoon chili flakes

Directions

1. In the air fryer pan mix up kohlrabi, heavy cream, salt, Cheddar cheese, water, and chili flakes.
2. Then preheat the air fryer to 255F.

3. Cook the meal for 20 minutes.

Nutrition value/serving: calories 71, fat 5, fiber 2, carbs 3.8, protein 3.4

Buttery Rutabaga

Prep time: 15 minutes | Cooking time: 8 minutes | Servings: 2

Ingredients:

- 6 oz rutabaga, chopped
- 2 oz Cheddar cheese, grated
- 1 tablespoon butter
- ½ teaspoon dried dill
- ½ teaspoon salt
- ½ teaspoon dried garlic
- 3 tablespoons heavy cream

Directions

1. In the mixing bowl mix up a rutabaga, dried dill, salt, and dried garlic.
2. Then add heavy cream and mix up the vegetables well.
3. After this, preheat the air fryer to 375F.
4. Put the rutabaga mixture in the air fryer and cook it for 6 minutes.
5. Then stir it well and top with grated cheese.
6. Cook the meal for 2 minutes more.
7. Transfer the cooked rutabaga in the plates and top with butter.

Nutrition value/serving: calories 275, fat 23.7, fiber 2.2, carbs 8.3, protein 8.7

Oregano Jicama Sticks

Prep time: 15 minutes | Cooking time: 7 minutes | Servings: 5

Ingredients:

- 15 oz jicama, peeled
- ½ teaspoon salt
- ½ teaspoon dried oregano
- ½ teaspoon chili flakes
- 1 teaspoon olive oil

Directions

1. Preheat the air fryer to 400F.
2. Cut jicama into the small sticks and sprinkle with salt, oregano, and chili flakes.
3. Then put the jicama stick in the air fryer and sprinkle with olive oil.
4. Cook the vegetables for 4 minutes.
5. Then shake them well and cook for 3 minutes.

Nutrition value/serving: calories 41, fat 1, fiber 4.2, carbs 7.6, protein 0.6

Scallop Squash Strips

Prep time: 20 minutes | Cooking time: 5 minutes | Servings: 4

Ingredients:

- 12 oz scallop squash
- 1 teaspoon coconut oil, softened
- 1 oz Provolone cheese, grated
- 1 teaspoon olive oil
- ¼ teaspoon cayenne pepper

Directions

1. Make the thin strips from the scallop squash. Use the spiralizer for this step.
2. Then place the vegetable strips in the air fryer and sprinkle with olive oil.
3. Cook them for 5 minutes at 385F.
4. Transfer the cooked squash strips in the serving plates and sprinkle with coconut oil and cayenne pepper.
5. Then top the vegetables with Provolone cheese.

Nutrition value/serving: calories 60, fat 4.4, fiber 0, carbs 3.5, protein 2.8

Aromatic Taco Broccoli

Prep time: 10 minutes | Cooking time: 12 minutes | Servings: 4

Ingredients:

- 1-pound broccoli
- 1 teaspoon taco seasonings
- 1 tablespoon coconut cream
- 1 teaspoon olive oil

Directions

1. Chop the broccoli roughly and sprinkle it with taco seasonings and coconut cream.
2. Then sprinkle the broccoli with olive oil.
3. Preheat the air fryer to 400F.
4. Cook it for 12 minutes. Shake the vegetables every 3 minutes.

Nutrition value/serving: calories 57, fat 2.4, fiber 3, carbs 7.7, protein 3.3

Tender Vegetable Mash

Prep time: 15 minutes | Cooking time: 15 minutes | Servings: 2

Ingredients:

- 1 large eggplant, trimmed, peeled
- 1 teaspoon ground turmeric
- ¼ cup water
- 1 garlic clove, peeled
- ½ teaspoon salt
- 1 white onion, diced

- ½ teaspoon avocado oil

Directions

1. Sprinkle the eggplant with salt and avocado oil.
2. Put it in the air fryer and cook for 15 minutes at 390F.
3. Then cool the cooked eggplant gently and chop roughly.
4. Transfer it in the blender.
5. Add water, turmeric, garlic, and onion.
6. Grind the mixture until it smooth.
7. Transfer the cooked meal in the bowl.

Nutrition value/serving: calories 87, fat 0.7, fiber 9.6, carbs 14.7, protein 3.1

Asparagus with Cheesy and Spiced Coat

Prep time: 10 minutes | **Cooking time:** 6 minutes | Servings: 4

Ingredients:

- 12 oz asparagus, trimmed
- 2 eggs, beaten
- ¼ cup Cheddar cheese, shredded
- ½ cup almond flour
- 1 teaspoon olive oil
- 1 teaspoon salt
- 1 teaspoon Italian seasonings

Directions

1. In the mixing bowl mix up Cheddar cheese, Italian seasonings, almond flour, and salt.
2. Then dip the asparagus in the beaten eggs and coat in the almond flour mixture.
3. Repeat the same steps one more time and transfer the coated asparagus in the air fryer basket.
4. Cook the vegetables for 6 minutes at 395F.

Nutrition value/serving: calories 171, fat 13.2, fiber 3.3, carbs 6.7, protein 9.4

Green Beans Salad

Prep time: 10 minutes | **Cooking time:** 6 minutes | Servings: 2

Ingredients:

- 6 oz okra, sliced
- 3 oz green beans, chopped
- 1 cup lettuce, chopped
- 1 teaspoon lime juice
- 1 teaspoon sesame oil
- ½ teaspoon salt
- 2 eggs, beaten
- 1 tablespoon almond flakes
- Cooking spray

Directions

1. In the mixing bowl mix up sliced okra and green beans.

2. Add cooking spray and salt and mix up the mixture well.
3. Then add beaten eggs and shake it.
4. After this, sprinkle the vegetables with almond flakes and shake okra and green beans to coat them in the almond flakes.
5. Preheat the air fryer to 400F.
6. Put the vegetable mixture in the air fryer and cook it for 6 minutes. Shake the mixture after 3 minutes of cooking.
7. After this, mix up cooked vegetables with lettuce, lime juice, and sprinkle with sesame oil.
8. Shake the salad.

Nutrition value/serving: calories 132, fat 7.8, fiber 4.6, carbs 8.5, protein 8.3

Halloumi Cheese Kebabs

Prep time: 15 minutes | **Cooking time:** 14 minutes | Servings: 4

Ingredients:

- 10 oz halloumi cheese
- 1 zucchini
- 1 green bell pepper
- 1 teaspoon dried parsley
- 1 tablespoon olive oil
- ½ teaspoon salt
- 1 teaspoon chili flakes

Directions

1. Chop green pepper, and zucchini roughly.
2. Then chop halloumi.
3. Put all ingredients from the list above in the big bowl and shake well.
4. Then string the ingredients on the wooden skewers and place in the air fryer.
5. Cook the kebabs for 14 minutes at 400F. Flip the kebabs on another side after 6 minutes of cooking.

Nutrition value/serving: calories 306, fat 24.8, fiber 1, carbs 5.7, protein 16.2

Roasted Broccoli Head

Prep time: 15 minutes | **Cooking time:** 25 minutes | Servings: 4

Ingredients:

- 12 oz broccoli head
- 2 tablespoons coconut oil, melted
- 1 teaspoon ground turmeric
- ½ teaspoon salt
- ¼ teaspoon cayenne pepper
- 1 bacon slice, chopped

Directions

1. In the mixing bowl mix up coconut oil, ground

turmeric, salt, and cayenne pepper

2. Then fill the broccoli head with chopped bacon.
3. After this, brush the vegetable with melted coconut oil mixture generously.
4. Preheat the air fryer to 365F.
5. Put the broccoli head in the air fryer basket and cook it for 25 minutes.

Nutrition value/serving: calories 97, fat 6.8, fiber 2.4, carbs 6.1, protein 4.2

Tender Garlic Bulb

Prep time: 5 minutes | **Cooking time:** 10 minutes | **Servings:** 4

Ingredients:

- 2 garlic bulbs
- ½ teaspoon coriander seeds
- 1 teaspoon sesame oil

Directions

1. In the shallow bowl mix up coriander seeds and sesame oil.
2. Then brush the garlic bulbs with oil mixture and put them in the air fryer.
3. Cook the garlic for 10 minutes at 375F.

Nutrition value/serving: calories 18, fat 1.1, fiber 0, carbs 1.5, protein 0

Cauliflower Wings

Prep time: 15 minutes | **Cooking time:** 6 minutes | **Servings:** 4

Ingredients:

- 2 cups cauliflower florets
- ¼ cup heavy cream
- ½ teaspoon salt
- ½ teaspoon chili flakes
- 1/3 cup almond flour
- 1 tablespoon keto Buffalo sauce
- Cooking spray

Directions

1. Sprinkle the cauliflower florets with salt and chili flakes.
2. Then dip them in the heavy cream and coat in the almond flour.
3. Preheat the air fryer to 400F.
4. Put the cauliflower florets in the air fryer, spray with cooking spray, and cook them for 6 minutes.
5. When the cauliflower is cooked, transfer in the bowl and sprinkle with Buffalo sauce.

Nutrition value/serving: calories 53, fat 4.1, fiber 1.5, carbs 3.4, protein 1.6

Keto Blooming Onion

Prep time: 15 minutes | **Cooking time:** 8 minutes | **Servings:** 3

Ingredients:

- 1 big white onion, peeled
- 1 egg, beaten
- ½ teaspoon ground paprika
- ½ teaspoon salt
- ½ teaspoon ground cumin
- 2 tablespoons coconut flour
- Cooking spray

Directions

1. Trim the onion and cut into the blooming bites with the help of the blooming cutter.
2. Then sprinkle the onion bites with ground paprika, salt, and ground cumin.
3. After this, dip every onion bite in the egg and coat in the coconut flour.
4. Preheat the air fryer to 400F and put the onion bites inside.
5. Spray them with the cooking spray and cook for 8 minutes.
6. Shake the onion after 4 minutes of cooking.

Nutrition value/serving: calories 67, fat 2.5, fiber 3.2, carbs 8.1, protein 3.5

Cajun Broccoli

Prep time: 10 minutes | **Cooking time:** 15 minutes | **Servings:** 2

Ingredients:

- ¼ onion, chopped
- 1 cup broccoli, chopped
- 1 teaspoon Cajun seasonings
- 1 teaspoon olive oil

Directions

1. In the mixing bowl mix up all ingredients.
2. Then preheat the air fryer to 385F.
3. Put the mixture in the air fryer and cook it for 15 minutes. Shake the vegetables every 5 minutes.

Nutrition value/serving: calories 41, fat 2.5, fiber 1.5, carbs 4.3, protein 1.4

Aromatic Beans Fries

Prep time: 15 minutes | **Cooking time:** 5 minutes | **Servings:** 2

Ingredients:

- 8 oz green beans
- 1 egg, beaten
- 1 teaspoon ricotta cheese
- ¼ cup coconut flour

- ¼ cup coconut flakes
- ½ teaspoon ground black pepper
- ½ teaspoon salt
- ¼ teaspoon nutmeg
- 1 teaspoon sesame oil

Directions

1. In the mixing bowl mix up ricotta cheese, egg, nutmeg, and ground black pepper. Add salt.
2. In the separated bowl mix up coconut flakes and coconut flour.
3. Preheat the air fryer to 400F.
4. Dip the green beans in the egg mixture and then coat in the coconut flakes mixture.
5. Repeat the step one more time and transfer the vegetables in the air fryer.
6. Sprinkle them with sesame oil and cook for 5 minutes. Shake the vegetables after 2 minutes of cooking if you don't put green beans in one layer.

Nutrition value/serving: calories 136, fat 8.5, fiber 5.6, carbs 10.9, protein 5.8

Simple Okra

Prep time: 10 minutes | **Cooking time:** 10 minutes | Servings: 3

Ingredients:

- 9 oz okra, chopped
- 1 teaspoon ground black pepper
- 1 teaspoon olive oil

Directions

1. In the mixing bowl mix up chopped okra, ground black pepper, and olive oil.
2. Then preheat the air fryer to 385F.
3. Put the okra mixture in the air fryer and cook it for 5 minutes.
4. Then shake the vegetables well and cook them for 5 minutes more.

Nutrition value/serving: calories 49, fat 1.7, fiber 2.9, carbs 6.8, protein 1.7

Tender Brussels Sprouts Halves

Prep time: 10 minutes | **Cooking time:** 15 minutes | Servings: 5

Ingredients:

- 1-pound Brussels sprouts
- 1 teaspoon chili powder
- 3 eggs, beaten
- 3 tablespoons coconut flakes
- 1 teaspoon salt
- 1 teaspoon coconut oil, melted

Directions

1. Cut Brussel sprouts into halves and put them in the bowl.
2. Add chili powder, eggs, and salt.
3. Shake the vegetables well and then sprinkle them with coconut flakes.
4. Shake the vegetables well.
5. Preheat the air fryer to 385F.
6. Put Brussel sprouts in the air fryer, sprinkle with the coconut oil, and cook them for 10 minutes.
7. Then shake the vegetables well and cook for 5 minutes more.

Nutrition value/serving: calories 97, fat 4.9, fiber 3.9, carbs 8.9, protein 6.6

Keto Falafel

Prep time: 15 minutes | **Cooking time:** 12 minutes | Servings: 4

Ingredients:

- 1 cup broccoli, shredded
- 1 teaspoon coconut flour
- ½ teaspoon ground cumin
- ¼ teaspoon ground coriander
- ½ teaspoon garlic, minced
- ½ teaspoon salt
- ¼ teaspoon cayenne pepper
- 1 egg, beaten
- 1 teaspoon tahini paste
- 2 tablespoons flax meal
- ½ teaspoon sesame oil

Directions

1. In the mixing bowl mix up shredded broccoli, coconut flour, ground cumin, coriander, garlic, salt, and cayenne pepper.
2. Add egg and flax meal and stir the mixture until homogenous with the help of the spoon.
3. After this, make the medium size balls (falafel) and press them gently.
4. Preheat the air fryer to 375F.
5. Put the falafel in the air fryer and sprinkle with sesame oil.
6. Cook the falafel for 6 minutes from each side.
7. Sprinkle the cooked falafel with tahini paste.

Nutrition value/serving: calories 55, fat 3.8, fiber 2, carbs 3.5, protein 3.1

Carrot Cakes

Prep time: 15 minutes | **Cooking time:** 8 minutes | Servings: 4

Ingredients:

- 1 carrot, grated
- ½ white onion, diced
- 1 cup cauliflower, shredded

- ½ teaspoon salt
- ½ teaspoon chili flakes
- 1 teaspoon ground paprika
- 1 egg, beaten
- ¼ cup coconut flour
- 1 teaspoon chives, chopped

Directions

1. In the mixing bowl mix up grated carrot, onion, shredded cauliflower, salt, chili flakes, ground paprika, and chives.
2. After this, add egg and stir the mixture with the help of the spoon.
3. Add coconut flour and stir it well again.
4. Make the cakes from the carrot mixture with the help of the fingertips.
5. Then preheat the air fryer to 385F and put the patties in the air fryer basket.
6. Cook them for 4 minutes from each side.

Nutrition value/serving: calories 39, fat 1.3, fiber 1.8, carbs 5, protein 2.4

Broccoli Rice Balls

Prep time: 15 minutes | **Cooking time:** 5 minutes | **Servings:** 2

Ingredients:

- 1 cup broccoli, shredded
- 3 oz Mozzarella, shredded
- 1 egg yolk
- 1 tablespoon almond flour
- ½ teaspoon salt
- ½ teaspoon ground black pepper
- 1 teaspoon ricotta cheese
- 1 teaspoon sesame oil

Directions

1. In the mixing bowl mix up shredded broccoli, shredded Mozzarella, egg yolk, almond flour, salt, ground black pepper, and ricotta cheese.
2. Stir the mixture until it is smooth.
3. With the help of 2 spoons make the balls.
4. Preheat the air fryer to 400F.
5. Put the balls in the air fryer and sprinkle them with sesame oil.
6. Cook the broccoli rice balls for 5 minutes.

Nutrition value/serving: calories 208, fat 14.1, fiber 1.7, carbs 6.1, protein 15.7

Vegetable Gnocchi

Prep time: 15 minutes | **Cooking time:** 4 minutes | **Servings:** 4

Ingredients:

- 2 cups broccoli, boiled
- 2 oz parmesan, grated
- 1 egg yolk
- 1 teaspoon ground white pepper
- 1 teaspoon ricotta cheese
- 3 tablespoons coconut flour
- 1 tablespoon butter
- 1 teaspoon dried cilantro

Directions

1. Put the boiled broccoli in the blender and grind it until you get the smooth mixture.
2. Then squeeze the broccoli to get rid of the water and transfer in the bowl.
3. Add grated Parmesan, egg yolk, ground white pepper, ricotta cheese, and coconut flour.
4. Knead the dough.
5. Then make the log and cut it into pieces (gnocchi).
6. Preheat the air fryer to 390F.
7. Put the gnocchi in the air fryer in one layer and cook them for 4 minutes.
8. Meanwhile, in the mixing bowl mix up butter and dried cilantro.
9. Microwave the mixture until it is melted.
10. When the gnocchi is cooked, place them in the plate and top with the melted butter mixture.

Nutrition value/serving: calories 148, fat 8.8, fiber 5.1, carbs 10.1, protein 8.2

Portobello Mushroom Cutlets

Prep time: 10 minutes | **Cooking time:** 5 minutes | **Servings:** 4

Ingredients:

- 4 Portobello mushroom caps
- 4 teaspoons sesame oil
- 1 teaspoon garlic powder

Directions

1. Trim the mushrooms if needed.
2. Preheat the air fryer to 400F.
3. In the mixing bowl mix up oil and garlic powder.
4. Sprinkle the mushrooms with garlic mixture and put in the how air fryer.
5. Cook the mushroom steaks for 5 minutes.

Nutrition value/serving: calories 50, fat 4.6, fiber 0.5, carbs 1.9, protein 0.8

DESSERT
RECIPES

Dessert Recipes

Almond Cupcakes

Prep time: 5 minutes | **Cooking time:** 25 minutes | Servings: 4

Ingredients:

- 1/3 ccup almond flour
- ½ cup cocoa powder
- 3 tablespoons stevia
- ½ teaspoon baking soda
- 1 teaspoon baking powder
- 4 eggs, whisked
- 1 teaspoon vanilla extract
- 4 tablespoons butter, melted
- ¼ cup coconut milk
- Cooking spray

Directions

1. In a bowl, mix all the ingredients except the cooking spray and whisk well. Grease a cupcake tin that fits the air fryer with the cooking spray.
2. Pour the cupcake mix, put the pan in your air fryer, cook at 350F for 25 minutes, cool down and serve.

Nutrition value/serving: calories 282, fat 25.7, fiber 4.6, carbs 9.8, protein 10

Lime Muffins

Prep time: 15 minutes | **Cooking time:** 11 minutes | Servings: 6

Ingredients:

- 1 cup coconut flour
- 3 tablespoons Erythritol
- 1 scoop protein powder
- 1 teaspoon vanilla extract
- 3 tablespoons butter, melted
- 1 egg, beaten
- ½ teaspoon baking powder
- ½ teaspoon instant coffee
- 1 teaspoon lime juice
- 2 tablespoons coconut cream
- Cooking spray

Directions

1. In the mixing bowl mix up coconut flour, Erythritol, protein powder, vanilla extract, butter, egg, baking powder, instant coffee, lime juice, and coconut cream.
2. With the help of the immersion blender, whisk the mixture until you get a smooth batter. After this, preheat the air fryer to 360F. Spray the muffin molds with cooking spray.
3. Then fill ½ part of every muffin mold with muffin batter and transfer them in the air fryer basket. Cook the muffins for 11 minutes.

Nutrition value/serving: calories175 fat 10, fiber 8.1, carbs 14.6, protein 7.5

Coconut Cookies

Prep time: 5 minutes | **Cooking time:** 15 minutes | Servings: 8

Ingredients:

- 1 and ½ cups coconut shred, unsweetened
- 2 tablespoons swerve
- ½ teaspoon baking powder
- ¼ teaspoon almond extract
- 2 eggs, whisked

Directions

1. In a bowl, mix all the ingredients and whisk well.
2. Scoop 8 servings of this mix on a baking sheet that fits the air fryer which you've lined with parchment paper.
3. Put the baking sheet in your air fryer and cook at 350 degrees F for 15 minutes. Serve cold.

Nutrition value/serving: calories 54, fat 4.8, fiber 0.9, carbs 1.6, protein 1.8

Buttery Muffins

Prep time: 15 minutes | **Cooking time:** 10 minutes | Servings: 2

Ingredients:

- 1 teaspoon of cocoa powder
- 2 tablespoons almond flour
- 2 teaspoons Erythritol
- ½ teaspoon vanilla extract
- 2 teaspoons butter, melted
- ¼ teaspoon baking powder
- 1 teaspoon apple cider vinegar
- ¼ teaspoon ground cinnamon

Directions

1. In the mixing bowl mix up cocoa powder, almond flour, Erythritol, vanilla extract, butter, baking powder, and apple cider vinegar.
2. Then add ground cinnamon and stir the mixture with the help of the spoon until it is smooth. Pour the brownie mixture in the muffin molds and leave for 10 minutes to rest.
3. Meanwhile, preheat the air fryer to 365F. Put the muffins in the air fryer basket and cook them for 10 minutes.

Nutrition value/serving: calories 201, fat 17.9, fiber 3.4, carbs 7.2, protein 6.2

Raspberries Cookies

Prep time: 15 minutes | **Cooking time:** 9 minutes | Servings: 4

Ingredients:

- 2 teaspoons coconut oil, softened
- 1 tablespoon Splenda
- 1 egg yolk
- ½ cup coconut flour
- 1 oz raspberries, mashed

Directions

1. In the mixing bowl mix up coconut oil, Splenda, egg yolk, and coconut flour. Knead the non-sticky dough.
2. Then make the small balls from the dough. Use your finger to make small holes in every ball.
3. Then fill the balls with mashed strawberries. Preheat the air fryer to 360F. Line the air fryer basket with baking paper and put the cookies inside.
4. Cook them for 9 minutes.

Nutrition value/serving: calories 112, fat 5, fiber 6.5, carbs 14, protein 2.8

Coconut Almonds

Prep time: 5 minutes | **Cooking time:** 40 minutes | Servings: 12

Ingredients:

- 1 and ¼ cups coconut flour
- 1 cup swerve
- 1 cup coconut oil, melted
- ½ cup coconut cream
- 1 and ½ cups coconut, flaked
- 1 egg yolk
- ¾ cup almonds, chopped
- ½ teaspoon vanilla extract

Directions

1. In a bowl, mix the coconut flour with half of the swerve and half of the coconut oil, stir well and press this on the bottom of a baking pan that fits the air fryer.
2. Introduce this mixture in the air fryer and cook at 350 F for 15 minutes.
3. Meanwhile, heat up a pan with the rest of the coconut oil over medium heat, add the remaining swerve and the rest of the ingredients, whisk, cook for 1-2 minutes, take off the heat and cool down.
4. Spread this well over the crust, put the pan in the air fryer again and cook at 350F for 25 minutes. Cool down, cut into bars and serve.

Nutrition value/serving: calories 304, fat 28.5, fiber 6.9, carbs 11.8, protein3.7

Lime Butter Bars

Prep time: 10 minutes | **Cooking time:** 35 minutes | Servings: 8

Ingredients:

- ½ cup butter, melted
- 1 cup erythritol
- 1 ¾ cups coconut flour
- 3 eggs, whisked
- Zest of 1 lime, grated
- Juice of 3 limes

Directions

1. In a bowl, mix 1 cup coconut flour with half of the erythritol and the butter, stir well and press into a baking dish that fits the air fryer lined with parchment paper.
2. Put the dish in your air fryer and cook at 350 F for 10 minutes.
3. Meanwhile, in a bowl, mix the rest of the flour with the remaining erythritol and the other ingredients and whisk well. Spread this over the crust, put the dish in the air fryer once more and cook at 350F for 25 minutes.
4. Cool down and cut into bars.

Nutrition value/serving: calories 230, fat 15.8, fiber 10.5, carbs 7.6, protein 5.7

Hazelnut Bars

Prep time: 15 minutes | **Cooking time:** 30 minutes | Servings: 10

Ingredients:

- ½ cup butter, softened
- 1 teaspoon baking powder
- 1 teaspoon apple cider vinegar
- 1 cup almond flour
- ½ cup coconut flour
- 3 tablespoons Erythritol
- 1 teaspoon vanilla extract
- 2 eggs, beaten
- 2 oz hazelnuts, chopped
- 1 oz macadamia nuts, chopped
- Cooking spray

Directions

1. In the mixing bowl mix up butter and baking powder. Add apple cider vinegar, almond flour, coconut flour, Erythritol, vanilla extract, and eggs.
2. Stir the mixture until it is smooth or use the immersion blender for this step. Then add hazelnuts and macadamia nuts.
3. Stir the mixture until homogenous. After this, preheat the air fryer to 325F.
4. Line the air fryer basket with baking paper. Then

pour the nut mixture in the air fryer basket and flatten it well with the help of the spatula. Cook the mixture for 30 minutes.

5. Then cool the mixture well and cut it into the serving bars.

Nutrition value/serving: calories 192, fat 17.7, fiber 3.5, carbs 6.3, protein 3.7

Sweet and Sour Zucchini Bread

Prep time: 10 minutes | **Cooking time:** 40 minutes | **Servings:** 12

Ingredients:

- 2 cups coconut flour
- 2 teaspoons baking powder
- ¾ cup swerve
- ½ cup butter, melted
- 1 teaspoon lime juice
- 1 teaspoon vanilla extract
- 3 eggs, whisked
- 1 cup zucchini, shredded
- 1 tablespoon lime zest
- Cooking spray

Directions

1. In a bowl, mix all the ingredients except the cooking spray and stir well.
2. Grease a loaf pan that fits the air fryer with the cooking spray, and pour the loaf mixture inside.
3. Put the pan in the air fryer and cook at 330 degrees F for 40 minutes. Cool down, slice and serve.

Nutrition value/serving: calories 167, fat 10.8, fiber 8.2, carbs 10.3, protein 4.3

Grapefruit Muffins

Prep time: 10 minutes | **Cooking time:** 10 minutes | **Servings:** 5

Ingredients:

- 5 eggs, beaten
- 1 tablespoon poppy seeds
- 1 teaspoon vanilla extract
- ¼ teaspoon ground nutmeg
- ½ teaspoon baking powder
- ¼ cup Grapefruit juice
- 1 teaspoon grapefruit zest, grated
- 5 tablespoons almond flour
- 1 tablespoon Monk fruit
- 2 tablespoons coconut flakes
- Cooking spray

Directions

1. In the mixing bowl mix up eggs, poppy seeds, vanilla extract, ground nutmeg, baking powder, grapefruit juice, grapefruit zest, almond flour, and

Monk fruit.

2. Add coconut flakes and mix up the mixture until it is homogenous and without any clumps. Preheat the air fryer to 360F.
3. Spray the muffin molds with cooking spray from inside. Pour the muffin batter in the molds and transfer them in the air fryer.
4. Cook the muffins for 10 minutes.

Nutrition value/serving: calories 87, fat 5.9, fiber 0.5, carbs 2.4, protein 6

Orange Pie

Prep time: 10 minutes | **Cooking time:** 35 minutes | **Servings:** 8

Ingredients:

- 2 eggs, whisked
- ¾ cup Erythritol
- ¼ cup almond flour
- 2 tablespoons coconut oil, melted
- 1 teaspoon orange zest, grated
- 1 teaspoon baking powder
- 1 teaspoon vanilla extract
- ½ teaspoon lemon extract
- 4 ounces coconut, shredded
- Cooking spray

Directions

1. In a bowl, combine all the ingredients except the cooking spray and stir well.
2. Grease a pie pan that fits the air fryer with the cooking spray, pour the mixture inside, put the pan in the air fryer and cook at 360F for 35 minutes.

Nutrition value/serving: calories 103, fat 9.7, fiber 1.4, carbs 25.4, protein 2.1

Ricotta Cheese Scones

Prep time: 20 minutes | **Cooking time:** 10 minutes | **Servings:** 4

Ingredients:

- 4 oz coconut flour
- ½ teaspoon baking powder
- 1 teaspoon apple cider vinegar
- ¼ teaspoon salt
- 2 teaspoons ricotta cheese
- ¼ cup heavy cream
- 1 teaspoon vanilla extract
- 1 tablespoon Erythritol
- Cooking spray

Directions

1. In the mixing bowl mix up coconut flour, baking powder, apple cider vinegar, and salt. Add ricotta cheese and stir the mixture gently. Mix up vanilla

extract and heavy cream in the separated bowl.

2. Stir it gently and then knead the dough. Roll up the dough and cut it on squares (scones).
3. Preheat the air fryer to 360F. Spray the air fryer basket with cooking spray and put the scones inside air fryer in one layer.
4. Cook the scones for 10 minutes or until they are light brown.
5. Then cool the scones to the room temperature.
6. Sprinkle the cooked dessert with Erythritol.

Nutrition value/serving: calories 93, fat 5, fiber 5, carbs 8.8, protein 2.4

Nutmeg and Orange Pie

Prep time: 5 minutes | **Cooking time:** 20 minutes | Servings: 8

Ingredients:

- 5 egg whites
- 1/3 cup Erythritol
- 1 ½ cups coconut flour
- Zest of 1 orange, grated
- 1 teaspoon baking powder
- 1 teaspoon vanilla extract
- 1/3 cup coconut oil, melted
- 2 cups strawberries, sliced
- ½ teaspoon ground nutmeg
- Cooking spray

Directions

1. In a bowl, whisk egg whites well. Add the rest of the ingredients except the cooking spray gradually and whisk everything.
2. Grease a tart pan with the cooking spray, and pour the strawberries mix.
3. Put the pan in the air fryer and cook at 370F for 20 minutes.
4. Cool down, slice and serve.

Nutrition value/serving: calories 103, fat 9.3, fiber 0.8, carbs 3.4, protein 9.3

Creamy Almond Cake

Prep time: 20 minutes | **Cooking time:** 40 minutes | Servings: 8

Ingredients:

- ½ cup heavy cream
- 3 eggs, beaten
- 3 tablespoons cocoa powder
- 1 teaspoon vanilla extract
- 1 teaspoon baking powder
- 3 tablespoons Erythritol
- 1 cup coconut flour
- 2 oz almonds, chopped

- 1 tablespoon sesame oil
- 1 teaspoon Splenda

Directions

1. Mix up heavy cream and eggs in the bowl. Add cocoa powder and stir the liquid until it is smooth.
2. After this, add vanilla extract, baking powder, Erythritol, coconut flour, almonds, ground nutmeg, and sesame oil.
3. Whisk the mixture gently and pour it in the cake mold.
4. Then cover the cake with foil. Secure the edges of the foil.
5. Then pierce the foil with the help of the toothpick.
6. Preheat the air fryer to 360F. Put the cake mold in the air fryer and cook it for 40 minutes. When the cake is cooked, remove it from the air fryer and cool completely.
7. Remove the cake from the mold and then sprinkle with Splenda.

Nutrition value/serving: calories 115, fat 9.9, fiber 1.5, carbs 3.8, protein 4.1

Stevia Donuts

Prep time: 5 minutes | **Cooking time:** 15 minutes | Servings: 4

Ingredients:

- 8 ounces almond flour
- 2 tablespoons stevia
- 1 egg, whisked
- 2 and ½ tablespoons butter, melted
- 4 ounces heavy cream
- 1 teaspoon baking powder

Directions

1. In a bowl, mix all the ingredients and whisk well.
2. Shape donuts from this mix, place them in your air fryer's basket and cook at 37F for 15 minutes.

Nutrition value/serving: calories 405, fat 36.8, fiber 4.1, carbs 9.6, protein 10.1

Vanilla Donuts

Prep time: 20 minutes | **Cooking time:** 6 minutes | Servings: 4

Ingredients:

- 1 teaspoon ground cardamom
- ½ teaspoon vanilla extract
- ½ teaspoon baking powder
- ½ cup coconut flour
- 1 tablespoon Erythritol
- 1 egg, beaten
- 1 tablespoon coconut oil, softened
- ¼ teaspoon salt

- Cooking spray

Directions

1. Preheat the air fryer to 355F.
2. In the shallow bowl mix up vanilla extract, ground cardamom, and Erythritol.
3. After this, in the separated bowl mix up coconut flour, baking powder, egg, salt, and coconut oil.
4. Knead the non-sticky dough. Add more coconut flour if needed.
5. Then roll up the dough and make 4 donuts with the help of the donut cutter.
6. After this, coat every donut in the cardamom mixture. Let the donuts rest for 10 minutes in a warm place.
7. Then spray the air fryer with cooking spray. Place the donuts in the air fryer basket in one layer and cook them for 6 minutes or until they are golden brown.
8. Sprinkle the hot cooked donuts with the remaining cardamom mixture.

Nutrition value/serving: calories 109, fat 6, fiber 6.2, carbs 10.8, protein 3.4

Cardamom Cookies

Prep time: 10 minutes | **Cooking time:** 20 minutes | Servings: 12

Ingredients:

- 2 eggs, whisked
- 1 tablespoon coconut cream
- ½ cup butter, melted
- 2 teaspoons ground cardamom
- 2 ¾ cup coconut flour
- Cooking spray
- ¼ cup swerve

Directions

1. In a bowl, mix all the ingredients except the cooking spray and stir well.
2. Shape 12 balls out of this mix, put them on a baking sheet that fits the air fryer greased with cooking spray and flatten them.
3. Put the baking sheet in the air fryer and cook at 350F for 20 minutes.

Nutrition value/serving: calories 192, fat 4.7, fiber 11.1, carbs 8.8, protein 4.7

Peppermint Cake

Prep time: 15 minutes | **Cooking time:** 9 minutes | Servings: 2

Ingredients:

- 1 tablespoon cocoa powder
- 2 tablespoons butter, softened
- 2 tablespoons swerve

- 1 teaspoon peppermint
- 3 eggs, beaten
- 1 teaspoon spearmint, dried
- 4 teaspoons coconut flour
- Cooking spray

Directions

1. Preheat the air fryer to 375F. Melt the butter in the microwave oven for 10 seconds.
2. Then add cocoa powder and coconut flour in the melted butter.
3. After this, add Erythritol, peppermint, and spearmint.
4. Add eggs and whisk the mixture until smooth. Spray the ramekins with cooking spray and pour the chocolate mixture inside.
5. Then put the ramekins with lava cakes in the preheated air fryer and cook them for 9 minutes.
6. Then remove the cooked lava cakes from the air fryer and let them rest for 5 minutes before serving.

Nutrition value/serving: calories 228, fat 18.9, fiber 2.9, carbs 7.4, protein 9.6

Ginger Cookies

Prep time: 10 minutes | **Cooking time:** 15 minutes | Servings: 12

Ingredients:

- 2 cups coconut flour
- 1 cup swerve
- ¼ cup coconut oil, melted
- 1 egg
- 2 teaspoon ground ginger
- 1 teaspoon vanilla extract
- ¼ teaspoon ground cinnamon

Directions

1. In a bowl, mix all the ingredients and whisk well.
2. Spoon small balls out of this mix on a lined baking sheet that fits the air fryer lined with parchment paper and flatten them.
3. Put the sheet in the fryer and cook at 360F for 15 minutes.

Nutrition value/serving: calories 127, fat 6.9, fiber 8.1, carbs 13.8, protein 3.2

Sweet Cheese Balls

Prep time: 20 minutes | **Cooking time:** 4 minutes | Servings: 8

Ingredients:

- 2 eggs, beaten
- 1 teaspoon butter, melted
- 9 oz coconut flour
- 5 oz Mozzarella, shredded

- 1 tablespoon coconut oil
- 2 tablespoons swerve
- 1 teaspoon baking powder
- ½ teaspoon vanilla extract
- Cooking spray

Directions

1. In the mixing bowl mix up butter and Mozzarella. Microwave the mixture for 10-15 minutes or until it is melted. Then add coconut flour. Add swerve and baking powder. After this, add vanilla extract and stir the mixture.
2. Knead the soft dough. Microwave the mixture for 2-5 seconds more if it is not melted enough. In the bowl mix up butter and eggs. Make 8 balls from the almond flour mixture and coat them in the egg mixture.
3. Preheat the air fryer to 400F. Spray the air fryer basket with cooking spray from inside and place the bread rolls in one layer.
4. Cook the dessert for 4 minutes or until the bread roll is golden brown.
5. Cool the cooked dessert completely and sprinkle with Splenda if desired.

Nutrition value/serving: calories 224, fat 9.8, fiber 13.7, carbs 4.3, protein 11

Cinnamon and Blackberries Cupcakes

Prep time: 10 minutes | **Cooking time:** 20 minutes | Servings: 8

Ingredients:

- ¾ cup blackberries
- ¼ cup ghee, melted
- 1 egg
- ½ cup swerve
- ¼ cup coconut flour
- 2 tablespoons almond meal
- 1 teaspoon cinnamon powder
- 3 tablespoons ricotta cheese
- ½ teaspoon baking soda
- ½ teaspoon baking powder
- Cooking spray

Directions

1. In a bowl, mix all the ingredients except the cooking spray and whisk well.
2. Grease a cupcake pan that fits the air fryer with the cooking spray, pour the blackberry mix, put the pan in the machine and cook at 350 degrees F for 20 minutes. Serve the cupcakes cold.

Nutrition value/serving: calories 102, fat 8.6, fiber 2.4, carbs 4.7, protein 2.4

Mulberries Pop-Tarts

Prep time: 25 minutes | **Cooking time:** 10 minutes | Servings: 5

Ingredients:

- 2 oz mulberries
- ½ cup coconut flour
- 1 egg, beaten
- 1 tablespoon coconut oil, softened
- 1 tablespoon Erythritol
- ½ teaspoon baking powder
- 1 egg white, whisked
- Cooking spray

Directions

1. In the mixing bowl mix up coconut flour, egg, coconut oil, and baking powder.
2. Knead the soft non-sticky dough.
3. Then mash the mulberries and mix them up with Erythritol. Cut the dough into halves.
4. Then roll up every dough half into the big squares. After this, cut every square into 5 small squares.
5. Put the mashed mulberries mixture on 5 mini squares. Then cover them with remaining dough squares. Secure the edges with the help of the fork.
6. Then brush the pop-tarts with whisked egg white. Preheat the air fryer to 350F. Spray the air fryer basket with cooking spray.
7. Then place the pop tarts in the air fryer basket in one layer.
8. Cook them at 350F for 10 minutes. Cool the cooked pop-tarts totally and transfer in the serving plates.

Nutrition value/serving: calories 93, fat 4.8, fiber 5, carbs 9.5, protein 3.6

Orange and Berries Jam

Prep time: 10 minutes | **Cooking time:** 20 minutes | Servings: 12

Ingredients:

- ¼ cup swerve
- 8 ounces raspberries, sliced
- 1 tablespoon orange juice
- ¼ cup water

Directions

1. In a pan that fits the air fryer, combine all the ingredients, put the pan in the machine and cook at 380F for 20 minutes.
2. Divide the mix into cups, cool down and serve.

Nutrition value/serving: calories 11, fat 0.1, fiber 1.2, carbs 2.4, protein 0.2

Creamy Blackberry Cake

Prep time: 20 minutes | **Cooking time:** 30 minutes | **Servings:** 4

Ingredients:

- 3 eggs, beaten
- ½ cup almond flour
- ½ teaspoon baking powder
- 2 teaspoons swerve
- 1 teaspoon vanilla extract
- 1 tablespoon Truvia
- ½ cup heavy cream
- 1 oz blackberries, sliced
- Cooking spray

Directions

1. Make the cake batter: in the mixing bowl mix up beaten egg, almomd flour, baking powder, and swerve.
2. Add vanilla extract and stir the mixture until smooth. Then preheat the air fryer to 330F. Spray the air fryer baking pan with cooking spray and pour the cake batter inside.
3. Put the pan with batter in the preheated air fryer and cook it for 30 minutes.
4. Meanwhile, make the cake frosting: whip the heavy cream. Then add Truvia and stir it well.
5. When the cake is cooked, cool it well and remove it from the air fryer pan. Slice the cake into 2 cakes.
6. Then spread one piece of cake with ½ part of whipped cream and top with sliced raspberries. After this, cover it with the second piece of cakes.
7. Top the cake with the remaining whipped cream.

Nutrition value/serving: calories 190, fat 15.5, fiber 1.9, carbs 4.8, protein 7.6

Strawberry Cream

Prep time: 4 minutes | **Cooking time:** 20 minutes | **Servings:** 6

Ingredients:

- 2 cups strawberries
- Juice of ½ lime
- 2 tablespoons water
- 1 teaspoon vanilla extract
- 2 tablespoons Erythritol

Directions

1. In a bowl, mix all the ingredients and whisk well.
2. Divide this into 6 ramekins, put them in the air fryer and cook at 340F for 20 minutes.
3. Cool down the dessert.

Nutrition value/serving: calories 17, fat 0.1, fiber 1, carbs 3.8, protein 0.3

Blueberries and Vanilla Pies

Prep time: 25 minutes | **Cooking time:** 26 minutes | **Servings:** 6

Ingredients:

- 8 oz coconut flour
- 1 teaspoon vanilla extract
- ¼ teaspoon salt
- 2 tablespoons swerve
- 2 eggs, beaten
- 1 tablespoon butter, melted
- 1 tablespoon xanthan gum
- 1 teaspoon flax meal
- 2 oz blueberries
- Cooking spray

Directions

1. In the mixing bowl mix up vanilla extract, eggs, and butter.
2. Then add coconut flour, salt, xanthan gum, and flax meal. Knead the non-sticky dough and roll it up.
3. Then cut the dough on 6 pieces. Put the blueberries on every dough piece. Sprinkle the berries with swerve.
4. Fold the dough pieces to make the pockets and secure the edges of them with the help of the fork.
5. Preheat the air fryer to 350F. Place the hand pies in the air fryer in one layer (4 pies) and cook them for 13 minutes.
6. Then remove the cooked pies from the air fryer and cool them to the room temperature. Repeat the same steps with remaining uncooked pies.

Nutrition value/serving: calories 128, fat 6.2, fiber 7.8, carbs 13.2, protein 4.8

Coconut and Vanilla Chocolate

Prep time: 10 minutes | **Cooking time:** 7 minutes | **Servings:** 2

Ingredients:

- ¼ teaspoon vanilla extract
- 1/3 cup coconut milk
- 1 teaspoon coconut oil
- 1 tablespoon cocoa powder
- ½ oz dark chocolate
- 1 teaspoon Erythritol

Directions

1. In the big cup whisk together coconut milk and cocoa powder. When the liquid is smooth, add vanilla extract and Erythritol. Stir it gently.
2. Then add dark chocolate and coconut oil. Put the cup with chocolate mixture in the air fryer and cook it at 375F for 3 minutes.
3. Then stir the liquid and cook it for 4 minutes more.

Carefully remove the cups with hot chocolate from the air fryer. Stir the hot chocolate gently with the help of the teaspoon.

Nutrition value/serving: calories 157, fat 14.3, fiber 1.9, carbs 8, protein 2

Keto Jam

Prep time: 10 minutes | **Cooking time:** 30 minutes | **Servings:** 12

Ingredients:

- 3 cups strawberries
- ¼ cup Erythritol
- 4 tablespoons lime juice
- 4 tablespoons chia seeds

Directions

1. In a pan that fits the air fryer, combine all the ingredients and toss.
2. Put the pan in the machine and cook at 300F for 30 minutes.
3. Divide into cups and serve cold.

Nutrition value/serving: calories 28, fat 1.1, fiber 1.9, carbs 4.2, protein 0.8

Coconut and Almond Cake

Prep time: 5 minutes | **Cooking time:** 20 minutes | **Servings:** 8

Ingredients:

- 2 eggs
- 3 tablespoons swerve
- 3 tablespoons butter, melted
- ¼ cup coconut milk
- 4 tablespoons coconut flour
- 1 tablespoon cocoa powder
- 2 oz almond flakes
- ½ teaspoon baking powder

Directions

1. In a bowl, mix all the ingredients and stir well.
2. Pour this into a cake pan that fits the air fryer, put the pan in the machine and cook at 340 degrees F for 20 minutes.

Nutrition value/serving: calories 277, fat 23.7, fiber 5, carbs 8.9, protein 7.7

Pumpkin Muffins

Prep time: 15 minutes | **Cooking time:** 10 minutes | **Servings:** 6

Ingredients:

- ½ cup almond flour
- 1 teaspoon pumpkin puree
- ½ teaspoon baking powder
- ½ teaspoon pumpkin spices
- 1 egg, beaten
- 3 teaspoons swerve
- 2 tablespoons coconut oil, melted
- Cooking spray

Directions

1. In the mixing bowl mix up almond flour, baking powder, pumpkin spices, and swerve.
2. Then add pumpkin puree, egg, and coconut oil. Stir the mixture until you get the smooth batter.
3. After this, spray the muffin molds with cooking spray.
4. Pour the batter in the muffin molds. Preheat the air fryer to 325F. Transfer the muffin molds in the air fryer and cook them for 10 minutes.

Nutrition value/serving: calories 107, fat 9.7, fiber 1.1, carbs 2.4, protein 2.9

Recipe Index

Made in the USA
Monee, IL
12 October 2023

44497275R00055